# NON
# OBVIOUS

# ABOUT THE NON-OBVIOUS TREND SERIES

For the past seven years, the Non-Obvious Trend Report has been one of the most widely read curated annual predictions about business and marketing trends in the world – read or shared online by over 1 million readers and utilized by dozens of global brands.

Unlike other trend reports, each new annual edition features 15 original trend predictions alongside detailed insights on how to use those trends to evolve your business or fast track your career.

This is the ALL NEW 2017 Edition of the Wall Street Journal Best Seller and features completely revised and updated insights as well as 15 new trends for this year.

The original edition of Non-Obvious has been translated into 6 languages globally – with new translated editions being released throughout the coming year.

For more details about booking private workshops, keynote speaking engagements, training or custom print editions of books from the series, visit www.nonobviousbook.com or contact info@nonobviouscompany.com.

# PRAISE FOR THE *NON-OBVIOUS* TREND SERIES

"*Non-Obvious* is a sharp, articulate, and immediately useful book about one of my favorite topics: the future. Filled with actionable advice and entertaining stories, Rohit offers an essential guidebook to using the power of curation to understand and prepare for the future of business."

**—DANIEL H. PINK**
Author of *To Sell Is Human* and *Drive*

"There are very few books that I read hoping that no one else around me will. They're the books that are so insightful, so thought provoking and so illuminating that they provide powerful competitive advantage. *Non-Obvious* is one of those. Pass on it at your own peril."

**—SHIV SINGH**
SVP Global Head of Digital & Marketing Transformation at VISA and author of *Social Media Marketing For Dummies*

"This is one of those rare books that delivers insights that are both useful and help illuminate where business is going. It's a great read."

**—CHARLES DUHIGG**
Author of the bestseller *The Power Of Habit*

"The insights in Rohit's Non-Obvious Trends are an invaluable guide to understanding our customer's customer. His predictions are useful and highly anticipated within our group across the globe every year. As a B2B marketer and leader, this is one of my rare must-read recommendations for my entire team."

**—NAVEEN RAJDEV**
*Chief Marketing Officer, Wipro*

"It doesn't take a crystal ball to predict that digital is the future. Rather than tell you what you already know, Rohit sets his sights on something much more important: helping you adopt a more curious and observant mindset to understand the world around you. If you believe in a lifetime of learning, read this book!"

**—JONATHAN BECHER**
Chief Marketing Officer, SAP

"A lot of books promise to help you see things differently but Rohit's book actually delivers. His insightful blend of visual thinking and business strategy shows you how to find meaningful patterns that others miss. A real mind-opener."

**—SUNNI BROWN**
Author, Gamestorming and The Doodle Revolution

"Shatter your magic crystal ball, and toss out the tea leaves. In this book, Rohit shows us how and where to find the future trends that will shape your business, your brand, and even your own decision-making."

**—SALLY HOGSHEAD**
*NY Times* bestselling author of *How The World Sees You*

"For the last four years, Rohit has helped make the non-obvious obvious by spotlighting trends to help anyone prepare their business for the future. It gets better every year so if you haven't been reading, it's time to start."

**—RYAN HOLIDAY**
Author of *Trust Me I'm Lying* and *Growth Hacker Marketing*

"Lots of books tell you to "think different" but *Non-Obvious* is one of the few books that actually teaches you how to do it. Whether you are trying to persuade clients, motivate a team, or just impress a demanding boss —*Non-Obvious* can help you succeed. I've already purchased copies for my entire team."

**—JOHN GERZEMA**
*New York Times* best-selling author and social strategist

"The best books approach their topic with a spirit of generosity. Rohit's new book offers insight into the business and cultural trends that matter. And why they do. And what actions they might inspire. But more than that, it also generously teaches you how to develop your own process, for evaluating the trends that matter and those that don't. Also, it's well--written. Which makes it a joy (and not a chore!) to read!"

**—ANN HANDLEY**
Chief Content Officer, MarketingProfs

"The aim of many business books is to give a man a fish. Rohit generously goes one better—not by simply telling us what's working, but by showing us how to apply his thinking for ourselves."

**—BERNADETTE JIWA**
Bestselling author, award-winning blogger & keynote speaker

"Non-Obvious is simple, elegant and powerful - one of those intensely engaging books that I couldn't put down. Every year I use the ideas in this book to help my team see new opportunities and out think our competition."

**—HOPE FRANK**
Chief Marketing and Digital Officer, Kiosked

"Rohit Bhargava's "Likeonomics" is the gold standard on understanding the social economy. His new book had me at "predict the future" but there's much more than that in here. It's about seeing the world in a new way — plus a powerful argument for how curation can change your organization."

**—SREE SREENIVASAN**
Former Chief Digital Officer, The Metropolitan Museum of Art
Host, "@Sree Show" podcast on CBS @Playit network

"Rohit provides a goldmine of ideas and trends that will shape the future of marketing and product development. Read this book to get in front of the herd."

**—GUY KAWASAKI**
Chief Evangelist of Canva
Author of *The Art of the Start, 2.0*

"Our industry is all about the future – the future of kids, the future of schools, the future of education. In the admissions office, the ability to recognize and leverage that future is an indispensable skill. In Non-Obvious, Rohit provides us the tools we require to perform those functions with precision and get better at predicting what will be important tomorrow based on improving your observations of today."

**—HEATHER HOERLE**
Executive Director, The Enrollment Management Association

"Seeing things that others don't is perhaps the highest form of creativity that exists. Unlock the Non-Obvious approach and you can write your ticket to success in any field."

**—JOHN JANTSCH**
Author of *Duct Tape Marketing and Duct Tape Selling*

"Very few people understand the world of digital business better than Rohit and I have introduced my clients to his ideas for years. His new book is a must-read resource for learning to see patterns, anticipate global trends, and think like a futurist every day!"

**—GERD LEONHARD**
Author and Keynote Speaker Basel / Switzerland

"*Non-Obvious* should be called *oblivious* since that's how you'll be if this book isn't on your shelf. I actually wish some of Rohit's predictions won't come true ('Selfie Confidence'!? Nooo!) ... but usually they do. He's the best at this, and this book shows you why."

**—SCOTT STRATTEN**
Four time Best-Selling Author, including 2014 Sales Book of the Year: *UnSelling*

"Rohit Bhargava collects ideas the way frequent fliers collect miles. His infectious enthusiasm for trends and strategy is a recipe for success for your enterprise. In *Non Obvious*, he provides the solution to a problem business owners, entrepreneurs, heads of marketing, and CEOs have struggled with for years —how do you identify where the market is headed and be there first, ready to take advantage of it. Artfully lacing stories together to pull out simple, yet powerful trends, Rohit offers a blueprint for making trend identification a key component of your business strategy. The format of his book makes it easy for the novice to adopt these principles, and for the expert to glean pearls of wisdom. While the title is Non Obvious, your next step should be obvious —read this book today!"

**—JOEY COLEMAN**
Chief Experience Composer at Design Symphony

"In Non-Obvious Rohit shares valuable tips, tricks, methodologies and insightful curated trends to help readers navigate the future. Recommended!"

**—ROSS DAWSON**
Chairman, Future Exploration Network

"Non-Obvious is a powerhouse 'must read' for corporate executives, marketeers and product and service developers. Rohit Bhargava provides valuable, entertaining and easily understood sideways insights into critical trends shaping the near future. He lifts the lid on the myths surrounding the dark arts of trend prediction and offers very practical guidance on how to spot, curate and capitalize on Non Obvious trends."

**—ROHIT TALWAR**
Global Futurist and CEO Fast Future Research

# NON
# OBVIOUS

## How To Think Different,
## Curate Ideas &
## Predict The Future

## 2017

## ROHIT BHARGAVA

Best Selling Author of *Likeonomics*

IDEAPRESS
PUBLISHING

IDEAPRESS
PUBLISHING

*To my parents – for always giving me*
*a chance to see the world in my own way …*
*even if it wasn't always non-obvious.*

# CONTENTS

—·—

## PART I
## THE ART OF CURATING TRENDS

## PART II
## THE 2017 NON-OBVIOUS TREND REPORT

### CULTURE & CONSUMER BEHAVIOR TRENDS

### MARKETING & SOCIAL MEDIA TRENDS

### MEDIA & EDUCATION TRENDS

### TECHNOLOGY & DESIGN TRENDS

# PART III
# THE TREND ACTION GUIDE

# PART IV
# PREVIOUS TREND REPORT SUMMARIES
# (2011-2016)

# AUTHOR'S NOTE:
## THE 2017 EDITION – WHAT'S NEW AND NON-OBVIOUS?

On an ordinary Friday evening this past October, I was reminded of why I wrote this book.

After four years of digitally publishing 15 new trends every year in my "Non-Obvious Trend Report," in 2015 I decided to transform the 5th edition of the report into a full length book. That was the year *Non-Obvious* first came out in print and, to my delight, it struck a chord in organizations and readers globally.

Instead of just publishing the trend research that year, I also revealed some of the processes that my team and I had previously only shared in private client workshops or in my university classes for gathering ideas, finding intersections and learning to consistently see the patterns that others usually missed.

Sitting on the grass outside my boys' elementary school that idle Friday evening for an outdoor movie night, my realization came when we started watching the animated film *Ratatouille*. The tale is a classic outsider story of a rat named Remy who lives beneath the streets of Paris and has a passion for cooking.

Of course, no one wants a rat in the kitchen – but Remy is encouraged by the imagined voice of his hero, a late chef whose longtime motto was: "anyone can cook." It was the perfect reminder that the things we often prescribe as only the domain of experts may be within reach of anyone who has the right combination of passion and curiosity.

That idea inspires me every time I think of it, because it is empowering in a way that I always hope to be as a teacher and mentor. It is also particularly relevant when applied to the topic of trend predictions.

The future is new and sexy. It has always been and always will be. The future is where money is made and lives and culture are shaped. The future is irresistible. Of course, *predicting* that future seems like it should be impossible. What if I told you it is not only possible, but something you can learn to do for yourself?

Unlike other "Futurists," I have never focused on the long-term *possible* future. Instead, I research and write about the short term *certain* future. I call this "the accelerating present." **The real secret to predicting the future is getting better at understanding the present.**

That's the simple premise at the heart of this book and it means that I believe anyone can learn to predict what will come by honing his or her powers of observing what is already happening.

Aside from teaching you a step by step approach to do this (Part I of the book), this 2017 edition also features original research presenting 15 new Non-Obvious Trends that will change business in the coming year. If you are a new reader to this book series, it might be easy to dismiss this list of trends as an expiring collection of ideas destined to be obsolete every 12 months when replaced by the next edition comes out. The truth, as the readers of earlier editions of these trends can attest, is that this has never been the case.

**New trends don't make "old" trends irrelevant.**

Instead, from our research, we know that a trend will either continue to gain momentum... or it will not – but they usually move independently from one another. Some of the biggest trends changing the world of business today are ideas that we first identified and wrote about more than three years ago.

Trends like the *Rise Of Curation (2011)* predicting how content creation would be the wave of the future in marketing, or *Corporate Humanity (2012)* to describe the importance of brand authenticity as a way to build customer loyalty or *Powered By Women (2013)* to describe the global shift toward women taking leadership roles in business. Each of these, when first published, were ahead of their time – but today they don't seem nearly as contentious.

These same trends that were once reasonably described as "non-obvious" when they were first published have, over time, become closer to obvious… and in some cases even fundamental. They matter more than ever, but they are no longer a surprise.

To ensure that these trends are not abandoned before their time, last year I decided to include five previously published trends among the 15 curated for the report. The feedback on this choice from readers and clients was extremely positive, so you will see that technique repeated in this year's edition.

For each previously predicted trend, choosing to revisit and include it involved significant additional research, compiling new stories and often outlining some unexpected nuances or shifts in the meaning of the trend.

In addition, one of the trademarks of this trend series has been a consistently humble willingness to shine an honest lens on ALL 105 previous trend predictions since 2011 along with transparent ratings for how they fared over time. You will find those "Longevity Ratings" in Part IV of this book. Next year our plan is to add a ratings and review panel to allow readers like you to have input into how past (and current) trends are scored to add even more authenticity to the process.

Beyond the trend report, if you don't want to wait an entire year before reading these insights – you are also welcome to subscribe to my "Non-Obvious Insights Newsletter" where I share 5-7 surprising and underappreciated stories every week. It is a wonderful community of storytellers, innovators, leaders and thinkers – and I highly value the time they spend reading the email every week. To join, you can visit www.rohitbhargava.com/subscribe and I would be honored to have you on the list.

As an added incentive, all of my subscribers will also receive an exclusive "sneak peek" at my 2018 trend research nearly a month before it is publicly available and published.

Finally, if this book sparks any new ideas for you or just gets you to think differently... I would love to personally hear about your experience or have a dialogue about them!

I respond to all my emails, and I relish the chance to have a conversation with readers and leaders like you. You can reach me by email directly at rohit@nonobviouscompany.com or pick the social media platform of your choice (Twitter, Facebook, etc) to connect with me there instead.

My business card describes me as a trend curator, speaker, and "nice guy." I invite you to test that last claim for yourself and look forward to engaging with you digitally or perhaps at an event in the near future.

Thanks for reading this and enjoy the book!

*Rohit Bhargava*
*Washington DC*
*December 2016*

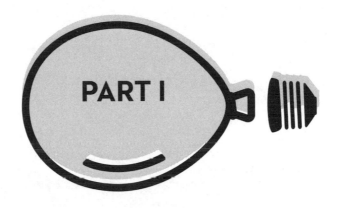

PART I

# THE ART OF TREND CURATION

# INTRODUCTION

·——·

## "I AM NOT A SPEED READER, I AM A SPEED UNDERSTANDER."

—ISAAC ASIMOV, Author, Historian and Biochemist

Isaac Asimov was not just a science fiction writer.

In his prolific lifetime, he wrote nearly 500 books on topics ranging from his beloved science fiction series to a two-volume work explaining the collected literature of William Shakespeare. He even wrote a reader's guidebook to the Bible.

Even though he was celebrated for his science fiction work, Asimov never defined himself in one category. When asked which his favorite book was, he often joked, "the last one I've written." He wasn't a scientist or a theologian or a literary critic. He was simply a writer with an incredible curiosity for ideas.

Unlike other experts, he knew that the power of his thinking came from his ability to bring disparate bodies of knowledge together and add his own insight. In fact, he used to describe himself as a "speed understander," a skill he clearly relied on to help him maintain a grueling schedule of publishing more than 15 books a year at his peak.

What if each of us could become a "speed understander" like Asimov? I believe we can.

The simple aim of this book is to teach you how to see the things that others miss. I call that "non-obvious" thinking, and learning how to do it can change your business and your career.

The context within which I'll talk about this type of thinking is business trends. For better or worse, most of us are fascinated by trends and those who predict them. We see these annual predictions as a glimpse into the future and they capture our imagination.

There's only one problem—most of them are based on guesswork or lazy thinking. They are *obvious* instead of *non-obvious*.

This book was inspired by the landslide of obvious ideas we see published today.

In a world where anyone is one button away from being a self-declared expert, learning to think differently is more important than ever. Observing and curating ideas can lead to a unique understanding of why people choose to buy, sell or believe anything.

This book aims to teach you the skills to avoid the obvious and see the ideas, patterns and trends that others miss.

---

**A great trend is a unique curated observation about the accelerating present.**

---

Great trends are never predictions about the world 20 years from now. Those are most often guesses or wishful thinking. How many trend forecasters do you think predicted the rise of something like Twitter back in 1997? Exactly zero.

Yet this doesn't mean trends are useless. The most powerful trends can offer predictions for the *short-term future* based on observing the present. And knowing the short-term future is more valuable than you may think.

## Why Does Trend Curation Matter?

Most of our life decisions happen in the short term, though we may describe them differently. You choose to start a business in the short term. You choose whom to marry in the short term. You change careers from one role to the next, all in the short term.

Long-term decisions start in the short term, so understanding how the world is changing in real time is far more valuable immediately than trying to guess what will happen in the world 20 years from now.

When I speak on stage, I often describe myself first as a "trend curator." The reason I use that term is because it describes my passion for collecting ideas and taking the time to see the patterns in them to describe the world in new and interesting ways.

For the past six years, I have published a curated look at the 15 biggest trends that will shape the business world in the year to come. Each year it is called the *Non-Obvious Trend Report* and each edition is based on a year of research, conversation, thinking and writing.

Across that time, I have advised some of the largest brands in the world on business strategy, taught marketing courses at Georgetown University and spoken at events in 32 countries around the world.

All of this gives me the valuable chance to work in dozens of different industries and study media, culture, marketing, technology, design and economics with an unfiltered eye. Each year, I also read or review dozens of books, and buy magazines on everything from cloud computing to Amish farming methods.

**My philosophy is to collect ideas the way frequent fliers collect miles—as momentary rewards to use for later redemption.**

# Why I Wrote This Book

This "redemption" comes in the form of my annual trend report, but unlike many other trend forecasters simply sharing my annual report is only the beginning. If I really believe in the value of curating trends, and that anyone can learn to do it, then it is also important for me to share my process for how to do it.

So this book is divided into four sections.

Part I is dedicated to my methods of trend curation, which I have usually only shared in depth through private workshops or with my students in class. You will learn the greatest myths of trend prediction, five essential habits of trend curators and my own step-by-step approach to curating trends, which I call the Haystack Method.

Part II is the 2017 edition of the *Non-Obvious Trend Report*, featuring 15 new ideas that will shape business in the year to come. Each trend features supporting stories and research, as well as ideas for how to apply the trend to your own business or career.

Part III is filled with tips on making trends actionable, including a short description of workshops to bring trends to life. In this part, I also discuss the importance of anti-trends and how to use "intersection think-ing" to see the patterns between industries and stories.

Finally, Part IV is a new look at 105 previously predicted trends from the past six years along with an honest assessment and rating for how each one performed over time since it was originally predicted.

You can choose to read this book in the order it was published or you can skip back and forth between trends and techniques. Whether you choose to focus on my predictions for 2017 and how to apply them, or learning the techniques of trend curation and non-obvious thinking for yourself, this book can be read in short bursts or all at once.

Like Asimov, you don't need to be a speed *reader*.

Being a speed *understander*, however, is a worthy aspiration. It is my hope that this book will help you get there.

# THE NORWEGIAN BILLIONAIRE:
## Why Most Trend Predictions Are Spectacularly Useless

In 1996 Christian Ringnes was a billionaire with the ultimate first-world problem – he was running out of space.

As one of the richest men in Norway, Ringnes is well known as a flamboyant businessman and art collector whose family started the country's largest brewery more than a hundred years ago. In his hometown of Oslo, Ringnes owns several restaurants and museums, and donated more than $70 million for the creation of a large sculpture and cultural park, which opened in 2013.

In his heart, Ringnes is a collector. Over decades he has built one of the largest private collections of art in the world. Yet his real legacy may come from something far more unique: his lifelong obsession with collecting mini liquor bottles.

This fixation on mini liquor bottles began for Ringnes at the age of seven when he received an unusual gift from his father: a half-empty miniature liquor bottle. It was this afterthought of a gift that led him on a path towards amassing what is recognized today as the largest independent mini-bottle collection in the world with over 52,000 miniature liquor bottles.

Unfortunately, his decades-long obsession eventually ran into an insurmountable opponent—his late wife, Denise.

As the now legendary story goes, Denise wasn't too happy with the disorganization of having all these bottles around the house. After years of frustration, she offered him an ultimatum: either find something to do with all those bottles or start selling them.

Like any avid collector, Ringnes couldn't bear the thought of selling them, so he created a perfectly obvious solution based on his wealth and personality.

He commissioned a museum.

## "To Collect Is Human"

Today the Mini Bottle Gallery in downtown Oslo is one of the world's top quirky museum destinations, routinely featured in irreverent travel guides and global lists of must-see Scandinavian tourist attractions. Beyond providing a place for Ringnes to put all of his mini bottles, the gallery is also a popular event venue with an in-house restaurant.

It was this event space and restaurant that offered me my first personal introduction to Ringnes and his story. I was in Oslo for an event and the conference team had organized a tour and dinner at the Mini Bottle Gallery.

It lived up to its quirky reputation.

The entrance to the museum was a bottle shaped hallway leading into an open lobby with a champagne waterfall. As you moved from room to room, each featured its own composed soundtrack, customized lighting and unique smells.

*I have 52,500 different miniature bottles in a museum in Oslo. They're completely useless. But men, we like collecting. We like having things. That's human. Once you get fascinated by something, you want it and then you start collecting.*

—Christian Ringnes
(From interview in Arterritory.com magazine)

Only steps into the tour, it was clear the gallery was more than just stacks of bottles lined along the walls of a display case in random fashion. Like all great museum experiences, the rooms of the Mini Bottle Gallery had been carefully *curated*.

The mini bottles were grouped into intriguing themes ranging from a brothel themed Room of Sin with mini-bottles from the Dutch Red Light District, to a Horror Room featuring liquor bottles with trapped objects floating inside like mice and worms.

There was a Jungle Room, a Room of Famous Persons, and rooms themed around sports, fruits, birds, circus performers and the occult. There was even an entire room featuring the iconic porcelain series of the Delft Blue KLM houses, a series of tiny Dutch rowhouse-shaped liquor bottles given away to passengers by KLM Airlines for more than five decades.

Across all these rooms, the gallery typically has more than 12,000 bottles on display at any one time. The rest are stored in a bottle vault below the museum and available for display when needed.

## Adding Meaning to Noise

The Mini Bottle Gallery only displays about 20% of Ringnes' full collection at any time, and carefully keeps the rest in storage. This thoughtful curation makes the experience of seeing them valuable.

If you consider the amount of media any of us is exposed to on an average day, the quest to find meaning amongst the noise is a familiar challenge. Navigating information overload requires the same discipline as deciding what bottles to put on display so those that visitors see can tell a better story.

**Curation is the ultimate method of transforming noise into meaning.**

Without curation, the meaning would be lost and the experience incomprehensible.

## An Accidental Trend Curator

It was only on my flight home from Oslo after that event that I realized how important curation had become for my own work.

Just a few months earlier I had published the first edition of my *Non-Obvious Trend Report*, inspired by an idea to publish an article from the many ideas I had collected over the past year but never written about.

What I was already doing without realizing it was collecting intriguing ideas and saving them in perhaps the most disorganized way possible—by writing them down randomly, printing them out or ripping them out of magazines and keeping them in a folder on my desk.

In producing that first report, my ambition became to describe patterns in the stories I had collected that went beyond the typical obvious observations I was always reading online. My goal was to find and develop insights that others either hadn't yet noticed or that were not getting the attention they warranted.

---

**To get a different output, sometimes you need a different input.**

---

On that flight home from Norway, I realized that my accidental method for getting different input—collecting ideas for a year and waiting months before analyzing them—could actually be the very thing that would set my insights apart and make them truly non-obvious.

The *Non-Obvious Trend Report* (my annual list of 15 trends) was born from this desire to share under appreciated ideas and connect them together into predictions about the future.

## Science's Dirty Little Secret

Now, if you happen to be an analytical person, this process will hardly seem rigorous enough to be believable. How can collecting ideas and waiting possibly be a recipe for developing genuine insights? What about firsthand research? What about trend panels and using a global army of spotters? What about the *science*?

Well, it turns out science has a forgotten side that has little to do with devising experiments and far more to do with training your powers of observation.

When you think about the discipline that goes into scientific research and the many years of study that lead to a PhD, it is easy to see research as a task only performed by robot-like perfectionists. The truth of scientific research, just like the truth behind many equally complex areas of study, is that the people behind them are far more human than we tend to admit.

In early 2013, a PhD candidate named Beckie Port gathered and published 75 examples of scientists using the hilariously viral hashtag #overlyhonestmethods to share some brutally honest truths about the realities of scientific research.

Among the compilation of tweets Port shared online were these entertaining sound bites:

- "Samples were prepared by our collaborators at MIT. We assumed no contamination because, well... they're MIT #overlyhonestmethods" (@paulcoxon)
- "Our representative device is representative of the ones which didn't immediately explode. #overlyhonestmethods" (@ajdecon)
- "Barbados was selected as a case study because the authors had a naive hope that it might justify some fieldwork there. #overlyhonestmethods" (@mlkubik)
- "We used jargon instead of plain English to prove that a decade of grad school and postdoc made us smart. #overly-honestmethods" (@eperlste)

Trends, like science, are not always perfectly observed phenomena that fit neatly into a spreadsheet to be described. Yet this doesn't mean they don't have immense value.

Effective scientific research always involves great observation. Scientists learn to observe the results of their experiments and then work to describe them with hypothesis and proof as best they can.

There are many similarities between trends and science, but this is only half the story. Discovering trends takes a willingness to combine curiosity with observation and add insight to create valuable ideas that you can then test to ensure they are valid.

This is vastly different from the method we often mistakenly believe is behind most work with trends: "trend spotting." This phrase itself is a symbol of the many myths we tend to believe about those who predict or describe trends.

Let's explore the five most common of these myths.

## The 5 Myths of Trend Spotting

As a writer and speaker, I spend a lot of time seeking stories. When it comes to trends and predicting the future, the people who do this are often called "trend spotters."

---

**Despite what you may have heard, learning trend spotting is not the key to predicting the future.**

---

Unfortunately, this trend-spotter bias has created a commonly referenced unreasonable portrait of the type of person who can predict the future. Consider this lazy definition for what it takes to become a trend spotter:

> *To become a trend spotter, someone usually receives extensive education and training in the industry he or she is interested in working for. After receiving a thorough grounding in the mechanics and history of the industry, the trend spotter could start working in company departments which predicted trends, slowly working to the rank of an official trend spotter. (Wisegeek.com)*

The assumption that you need to be working in "company departments which predicted trends" is just plain idiotic – and wrong.

Anyone can learn the right habits to become better at curating trends and predicting the future for themselves. You just need to develop the right habits and mindset.

Before we start learning those habits, however, it is important to tackle the biggest myths surrounding trends and explain why they are so wrong.

## MYTH #1: TRENDS ARE SPOTTED.

The idea of trend spotting suggests that there are trends simply sitting out there in plain sight ready to be observed and cataloged like avian species for bird watchers. The reality of trends is far different. Trend spotters typically find individual examples or stories. Calling the multitude of things they spot the same thing as trends is like calling eggs, flour and sugar sitting on a shelf the same thing as a cake. You can "spot" ingredients, but trends must be curated from these ingredients in order to have meaning.

## MYTH #2: TRENDS ARE PREDICTED BY INDUSTRY GURUS/EXPERTS.

It is tempting to see industry expertise as a prerequisite to being good at curating trends, but there is also a predictable drawback: blind spots. Put simply, the more you know about a particular topic, the more difficult it becomes to think outside your expertise and broaden your view. There is no single expertise required to curate trends, but Psychologists and business authors have long referred to this as the "curse of knowledge" and we all have it about something. To escape this "curse" you need to learn to engage your greater curiosity about the world beyond *any* industry to avoid any danger of industry-based tunnel vision.

## MYTH #3: TRENDS ARE BASED ON HARD DATA.

When it comes to research, some people rely on only numbers inserted into a spreadsheet as proof and they conveniently forget that there are two methods to conducting research: the quantitative method *and* the qualitative method. Qualitative research involves using observation and experience to gather mainly verbal data instead of results from experiments. If you are uncovering the perfect pH balance for shampoo, you definitely want to use quantitative research. For curating trends, you need a mixture of both and the ability to remember that research data can often be less valuable than really good observation.

## MYTH #4: TRENDS ONLY REFLECT CURRENT POPULARITY.

The line between trends and fads can be tricky. Although some trends seem to spotlight a currently popular story, good ones need to describe something that happens over a span of time. Fads, in comparison, describe an idea that is popular in the short term. Great trends do reflect a moment in time, but they also describe more than a fleeting moment.

## MYTH #5: TRENDS ARE HOPELESSLY BROAD PREDICTIONS.

Perhaps no other myth about trends is as fueled by reality as this one. The fact is, we encounter hopelessly broad trend predictions in the media all the time. The problem comes in treating those as indications that trends *should* be broad and all encompassing. Good trends tend to be more of the opposite. They define something that is concrete and distinct. Something that doesn't apply to everyone, but rather offers a point of view that you can easily grasp and describe in a unique way.

Now that I have shared five of the most common myths about trend predictions, we need to spend a brief moment considering why so many trend predictions involve self-indulgent guesswork or lazy thinking. What exactly makes them so useless?

In order to illustrate, let me tell you a little story.

# Why (Most) Trend Predictions Are Useless

Last December I picked up the year end edition of *Entrepreneur* magazine which promised to illuminate trends to watch in the coming year. Earlier that same week, a special double issue of *BusinessWeek* magazine had arrived in the mail making a similar promise.

It was the end of the year and the trend season was in full swing.

Just like New Year's resolutions to lose weight, trend forecasting is popular in December. Unfortunately, the side effect of this annual media ritual is an abundance of lazy predictions and vague declarations.

For entertainment over the years, I have started to collect them as standing memorials to the volume of pitiful predictions that bombarded us at the end of every year.

To illustrate my point, here are a few of the worst offending most obvious "trends" shared near the end of last year. For the sake of kindness,

I removed reference to which particular publication or writer a trend came from before listing them below:

- "It's all about the visuals."
- "Streaming video content."
- "The Year Of Drones has arrived. Really."
- "Content Marketing will continue to be the place to be."
- "Fantasy Sports"
- "Virtual Reality"
- "Change will be led by smart home technology."

*Virtual Reality*? Really?

Not to ruin the suspense, but I don't believe any of these are actually trends. Some are just random buzzwords or the names of platforms. Others are hopelessly broad, useless and, yes, obvious.

None of them are a unique idea describing the accelerating present.

Meanwhile, all of us as media consumers see these predictions with varying levels of skepticism. To better understand why, let's review the four main reasons why most trend predictions fail the believability test.

## REASON 1: NO OBJECTIVITY

If you sell virtual reality content, declaring 2017 the "Year of Virtual Reality" is clearly self-serving. Of course, most bias isn't this easy to spot and objectivity is notoriously difficult for any of us. Our biases are based on our expertise and the world we know. This is particularly true in business where we sometimes *need* to believe in industry or brand in order to succeed. The problem is, losing objectivity usually leads to wishful thinking. Just because we want something to be a trend doesn't make it one.

*EXAMPLE: Near the end of last year, I received what seemed like dozens of emails about white papers and blog posts each forecasting that wearable technology or the "Internet of things" would be the hottest trend of the coming year. Unsurprisingly, the vast majority of them had some type of product or strategy to cash in on this hot trend—and were mostly dismissed by the media they were aiming to reach.*

## REASON 2: NO CREATIVITY

Trends need to do more than repeat common knowledge. For example, saying that "more people will buy smart phones this year" is obvious—and useless because it lacks creativity. The biggest reason that most trend predictions share these types of obvious ideas is because it is easier to do so. Lazy thinking is always easier than creative and informed thinking. Great trends are never obvious declarations of fact that most people already know. They share new ideas in insightful ways while also describing the accelerating present.

> *EXAMPLE: The phrase "digital natives" was first coined nearly 15 years ago to describe a generation who would grow up never having known a world before the Internet. Despite its long history and relative ubiquity, several trend articles still share the "emergence" of this group as if it were a brand new insight. That's just plain lazy.*

## REASON 3: NO PROOF

Sharing a trend without specific examples is like declaring yourself a musician by simply buying a microphone and learning to sing one song. Unfortunately, many trend predictions coast on the power of a single story or example. Great examples and stories are powerful parts of illustrating why a trend matters. They are necessary elements of proving a trend. Only finding one example and declaring something a trend without more evidence is usually a sign that a so-called trend is based on little more than guesswork.

> *EXAMPLE: When publishing website Medium.com first became publicly available and increasing numbers of journalists and writers began using it to freely share extremely high-quality stories and articles, several early trend reports last year predicted the rise of a sort of anti-Twitter trend where people would begin flocking to longer-form content. Unfortunately, one popular website isn't enough to describe a trend, and most of these forecasts were predictable failures.*

## REASON 4: NO APPLICATION

Perhaps the most common place where many trend predictions fall short is in the discussion of how to apply them. It is not enough to think about trends in the context of describing them. The best trend forecasts go further than just describing something that is happening. They also share insights on what it means and what you can or should do differently as a result of the trend. In other words, trends should be actionable.

*EXAMPLE: In a piece of accidentally ironic content, a collaboration of top PR agencies published a sponsored editorial in* Advertising Age *magazine last year aimed at sharing predictions for the upcoming year to underscore the value of PR for big clients. Unfortunately, most of the top ten predictions featured plentiful buzzword babble, like "Big data is important, but big insights are critical" and was dramatically short on any real insights on how to apply the thinking or what to do about it. Not the PR industry's best work.*

## How to Think Different about Trends

So if there are so many myths and reasons for failure, what makes a good trend?

As a reminder, here is my definition for a "non-obvious" trend:

---

**A non-obvious trend is a curated observation that describes the accelerating present in a new, unique way.**

---

The next two chapters will dig further into the idea of non-obvious trends and thinking by sharing a step-by-step approach to help you think differently about trends and escape the trap of lazy thinking or flawed insights visually. The biggest challenge is learning to abandon the obvious ideas and push yourself to work harder.

When you do, I guarantee that your ideas will improve, as well as your outlook on your business and your career as well.

So, let's get started.

# THE CURATOR'S MINDSET:
## Learning the 5 Essential Habits of Trend Curators

—•———•—

"YOU NEVER LEARN ANYTHING
BY LISTENING TO YOURSELF SPEAK."
—SIR RICHARD BRANSON, Entrepreneur and Founder of the Virgin Group

In 2006, renowned Stanford psychology professor Carol Dweck wrote a book about an idea so simple it hardly seemed worth mentioning—much less devoting an entire book to exploring.

Across decades of research into motivation, achievement and success, Dweck had come upon a beautifully elegant idea to describe why some people succeeded while others failed: it all came down to *mindsets.*

After conducting experiments with grade school students, interviewing professional athletes and studying business leaders, Dweck proposed that most people had one of two types of mindsets: a fixed mindset or a growth mindset.

People with *fixed mindsets*, Dweck argued, believe that their skills and abilities are set. They see themselves as either being either good at something or not good at something, and therefore tend to focus their efforts on tasks and in careers where they feel they have a natural ability.

People with *growth mindsets* believe that success and achievement are the result of hard work and determination. They see their own (and others') true potential as something to be defined through effort. As a result, they thrive on challenges and often have a passion for learning.

It likely won't surprise you to learn that I believe in the power of the growth mindset and aspire to always maintain one for myself. When it comes to learning to predict the future, it is important to adopt that same mindset for yourself.

---

**The beautiful thing about mindsets is that we all have the ability to change ours—we just need to make the choice to do it.**

---

Seeing trends, like playing an instrument or being more observant, are skills within your grasp to learn and practice. Does this mean you can transform yourself into a professional flamenco guitarist or a full-time trend forecaster with enough practice? Not necessarily. Aptitude and natural talent do play an important part in succeeding at anything on a professional level.

Still, my work with thousands of executives and students at all levels of their careers has proved to me that the skills required for trend curation can be learned and practiced. When you learn them, they can inform your own view of the world and power your own future success.

> As soon as children become able to evaluate themselves, some of them become afraid of challenges. They become afraid of not being smart. I have studied thousands of people ... and it's breath-taking how many reject an opportunity to learn.
>
> —Carol Dweck (from *Mindset*)

Beyond adopting the growth mindset and having a willingness to learn, there are five core habits that will help you develop your trend-curation abilities. Let's explore them by starting with a story of the most famous art collector most people had never heard of—until he passed away a few years ago.

## The Unlikely Curator

By 2012, at the ripe old age of 89 years, a retired postal worker had quietly amassed one of the greatest collections of modern art in the world.

Herbert Vogel and his wife, Dorothy, were already legends in the world of art when Herbert passed away. News stories soon after his death told the story of five large moving vans showing up at the Vogel's rent-controlled, one-bedroom New York apartment to pick up more than 5000 pieces of art. This Vogel Collection, built over decades, would have a permanent home as part of the archives and collection at the National Gallery of Art.

The Vogels always said the only things they did were buy and collect art they loved.

This passion often led them to find new young artists to support before the rest of the world discovered them. The Vogels ultimately became more than collectors. They were tastemakers and their "fabled collection," as one critic later described it, which included art from hundreds of artists including pop artist Roy Lichtenstein and post-minimalist Richard Tuttle, was the envy of museums around the world.

The same qualities that drive art patrons like the Vogels to follow their instincts and collect beautiful things are the ones that make great curators of any kind.

## The Rise Of "Curationism"

Museum curators organize collections into themes that tell stories. Whether they're quirky like those told in the Mini Bottle Gallery, or an expansive exhibit at the Metropolitan Museum of Art, the goal of curation is always to take individual items and examples and weave them together into a narrative.

---

**Curators add meaning to isolated beautiful things.**

---

I am inspired by curators—and I am clearly not alone. The business world has turned toward the longtime practice of curation with such growing frequency that even the world of artists and art critics has begun to notice.

In 2014, art critic and writer David Balzer published a book with the brilliant title *Curationism* (a play on creationism) to explore how "curating took over the art world and everything else." His book explores the evolution of the curator as the "imparter of value."

Along the way he shares the valuable caution that this rise in curationism can sometimes inspire a "constant cycle of grasping and display" where we never take the time to understand what all the pieces mean. In other words, curation is only valuable if you follow the act of collecting information with enough moments of "quiet contemplation" to truly understand what you are seeing and collecting.

This combination of collection and contemplation is central to being able to effectively curate ideas and learn to predict the future. To do it, there are five specific habits that I believe can help you use curation to better see what others don't.

## The 5 Habits Of Trend Curators

I realize that calling yourself a "curator" of anything can seem like a stretch. Curator is often a job title applied to someone who has years of expertise in something, and perhaps even limited to certain industries. Yet curators today can come from all different types of backgrounds.

Some focus on art and design while others may look at history or anthropology. Some have professional training and degrees while others are driven by passion like Herbert and Dorothy Vogel. No matter their background, every one of them exhibits the same types of habits that help them to become masters at adding meaning to collected items.

Curation doesn't require you to be an expert or a researcher or an academic. Learning these five habits will help you put the power of curation to work to help you discover better ideas and use them to develop your own observations about the rapidly accelerating present.

1. **BEING CURIOUS** – always asking why, investing in learning and improving your knowledge by investigating and asking questions.

2. **BEING OBSERVANT** – learning to see the small details in stories and life that others may ignore or fail to recognize as significant.

3. **BEING FICKLE** – moving from one idea to the next without becoming fixated, or overanalyzing each idea in the moment.

4. **BEING THOUGHTFUL** – taking time to develop a meaningful point of view and considering alternative viewpoints without bias.

5. **BEING ELEGANT** – seeking beautiful ways to describe ideas that bring together disparate concepts in a simple and understandable way.

For the past five years I have been sharing and teaching these habits through workshops and classes to business professionals, entrepreneurs and university students. Those experiences have taught me that we all have the aptitude to learn these skills.

To learn how let's start with the first habit: curiosity.

## How to Be Curious

Bjarni Herjulfsson could have been one of the most famous explorers in the history of the world.

Instead, his life has become a cautionary tale about the historic consequences of lacking curiosity. In the year 986, he set off on a voyage from Norway with a crew to find Greenland. Blown off course by a storm, his ship became the first European vessel in recorded history to see North America.

Despite his crew pleading to stop and explore, Herjulfsson refused and guided his ship back on course to eventually find Greenland. Years later, he told this tale to a friend named Leif Eriksson who became inspired, purchased Herjulfsson's ship and took the journey for himself.

As many of us learned in grade school, Eriksson is now widely remembered as the first European to land in North America—nearly 500 years before Christopher Columbus. Herjulfsson, on the other hand, has been mostly forgotten and his story illustrates one of the most compelling facts about curiosity: it is a prerequisite to discovery.

---

**Being more curious means asking questions about why things work the way they do and embracing unfamiliar situations or topics with a sense of wonder.**

---

Humans are naturally curious. The challenge is to continually find ways to allow yourself to explore your curiosity without it becoming an ongoing distraction.

When noted chef and food pioneer Ferran Adrià was once asked what he likes to have for breakfast, his reply was simple: "I like to eat a different fruit every day of the month."

Imagine if you were able to do that with ideas.

Part of being curious is wanting to consume stories, ideas and experiences to earn greater knowledge of the world, even if that knowledge doesn't seem immediately useful.

## REAL LIFE ADVICE (3 WAYS TO BE MORE CURIOUS TODAY)

- ✓ **Consume "Brainful Media"** – Sadly we are surrounded with "brainless media," including reality shows featuring unlikeable people doing unlikeable things (sometimes on islands, sometimes in our backyards). While often addictively entertaining, brainless media encourages vegetation instead of curiosity. Curiosity is fueled by consuming "brainful media," such as a short documentary film or inspirational 17-minute talk from TED.com instead.

- ✓ **Empathize with Magazines** – Curiosity helps you see the world through someone else's eyes, even if it is initially uncomfortable. One technique I often use is buying niche magazines to learn about unfamiliar topics. Simply walking into the magazine section of a bookstore offers plenty of options. For example, *Modern Farmer*, *Model Railroader* and *House Beautiful* are three vastly different magazines. Flipping through the stories, advertisements and imagery in each will do more to take you outside of your own world than almost any other quick and easy activity.

✓ **Ask Bigger Questions** – Last year I was invited to deliver a talk at an event for the paint industry. It is an industry I know very little about and so it was tempting to show up, deliver my keynote and then leave. Instead, I stayed and walked around the exhibit hall asking questions. In less than 30 minutes I learned about how paint is mixed and what additives are typically used. I heard about the industry debate between all-plastic cans versus steel and the rise of computerized color matching systems. As a result my talk was far more relevant because I chose to stay and ask more questions instead of taking the easy path.

## WHAT TO READ

✓ **Historical Fiction** – Every great piece of historical fiction was inspired by a writer who found a story in history that was worth retelling and sharing with the world. This curiosity makes books like Erik Larson's *The Devil In The White City* (about murder at the 1893 Chicago World's Fair) or Simon Winchester's *The Professor And the Madman* (about the creation of the *Oxford English Dictionary*) wonderful gateways to start thinking about the world in unexpected ways.

✓ **Curated Compilations** – There are many books that bring together real life stories or essays to help you think about new and interesting topics. A collection of shorter topics and stories is sometimes far easier to use for engaging your curiosity than a longer book. For example, the *This Will Make You Smarter* series edited by John Brockman or any book by *You Are Not So Smart* founder and psychology buff David McRaney are perfect, bite-sized ways to inspire your curiosity without requiring a huge time investment.

# How to Be Observant

A few years ago I was invited to a formal dinner at an event in New York. The venue was a beautiful restaurant and after our meal the waiter came around to take our dessert orders from one of two set menu options. Less than 10 minutes later, a team of six people *not* including our waiter came and delivered all the desserts to our large table of 30 people, getting each order perfectly right without saying a word to anyone.

As they delivered the desserts, I started to wonder how that one waiter who took our orders had managed to relay all those choices perfectly to a team of six in such as short time?

By observing, I quickly figured out the simple trick our head waiter had used. If you had picked dessert option one, he had placed a dessert spoon *above* your plate. And if you picked option two, he had placed the spoon to the *right* of your plate.

So when that team of food runners came to the table, all they needed was the "code" to decipher the spoon positioning and they would be able to deliver the desserts perfectly. That little story of food delivery is a perfect example of why observation matters.

---

**Being more observant means training yourself to see the details that most others often miss.**

---

Perhaps you already knew that little spoon trick, but imagine you didn't. Simply observing it could teach you something fascinating about the little processes that we rarely pay attention to that keep the world moving along. Of course understanding how dessert is delivered will hardly change your life, but imagine that moment multiplied by a hundred or a thousand.

Learning to be more observant isn't just about seeing the big things. Instead, it is about training yourself to pay more attention to the little things too.

By simply choosing to observe, what can you see about a situation that no one else notices?

What can that teach you about people, processes and companies that you didn't know before?

This is the power of making observation a habit.

## REAL LIFE ADVICE
## (3 WAYS TO BE MORE OBSERVANT TODAY)

✓ **Explain the World to Children** – If you are lucky enough to have children in your life, one of the best ways to train yourself to use observation more frequently is to get better about explaining the world around you to children. When my kids asked me recently why construction vehicles and traffic signs are orange but cars aren't, it forced me to think about something I would otherwise have easily ignored, even if I didn't have the perfect answer to the question.*

✓ **Watch Processes in Action** – Every situation is filled with processes, from how school buses drop off children at their stops to how coffee shops take and make orders every morning. When you look at these interactions, you'll notice that very little happens by accident. Pay attention and ask yourself what does a typical interaction look like? How does it differ when it involves a "regular" versus a "newbie"? Seeing these patterns in regular everyday life can help you train yourself to use this observational skill in other situations as well.

✓ **Don't Be Observationally Lazy** – It is easy to go through the mundane moments of life glued to your smartphone. Aside from being really good at capturing our attention, they also keep us from seeing the world around us. Rather than switching to auto-pilot to navigate daily tasks like commuting or buying groceries, train yourself to put your phone down and choose to be observant instead.

## WHAT TO READ

------

\* *In case you were wondering, they are orange because testing shows that is the color most visible from the greatest distance. And cars aren't because people care more about picking a color they like than optimizing their car for safety by making it orange.*

✓ *What Every Body Is Saying* **by Joe Navarro** – If you need to learn the art of interpreting body language or detecting lies, a former FBI agent like Joe Navarro is probably the ideal teacher. In this best-selling book from 2008, Navarro shares some of his best lessons on how to spot "tells" in body language and use them to interpret human behavior. His work on situational awareness and teaching people *how* to be more observant to assess people and situations for danger and comfort is a book that should be on your reading list no matter what you do. It also happens to be a perfect supporting book to teach you how to be more observant.

## How to Be Fickle

Being fickle may seem like a bad thing, but that isn't always true.

When we hear the word, we tend to think of all the negative situations where we abandon people or ideas too quickly, but there is an upside to learning how to be purposefully fickle.

---

**Being fickle means capturing ideas without needing to fully understand or analyze them in that same moment.**

---

On the surface, this may seem counterintuitive. After all, when you find a great idea why wouldn't you take the time to analyze it and develop a point of view? There are certainly many situations when you do this already.

But you probably *never* do the opposite. A part of becoming an idea curator is saving ideas for later digestion. Of course you can always think about them when you find them, but you don't always *need* to.

For example, here are three interesting stories which I recently saw and saved:

- Coca-Cola decided to disconnect voicemail for all employees at its corporate headquarters in Atlanta.
- Richard Branson allows Virgin staff to take as much holiday as they want.

- A Trader Joe's employee gave a gift of flowers to a flustered mom of adopted kids who was leaving the store after an embarrassing toddler meltdown because the employee herself had been adopted and she just wanted to say thanks.

When I saved each of the stories above, I didn't make the broader connection to tie them together. Only when I reviewed them at the end of the year while researching trends did I realize that each of these stories says something unique about the state of employee relationships with their employers and empowerment.

There was a theme, but it was only by setting those stories aside and choosing to analyze them later that I had enough perspective to see that connection. Being fickle isn't about avoiding thought—it is about freeing yourself from the pressure to recognize connections immediately and make it easier to save an idea for later analysis.

## REAL LIFE ADVICE (3 WAYS TO BE MORE FICKLE TODAY)

✓ **Save Ideas Offline** – Thanks to wonderful productivity apps like Evernote and other smart technology solutions, there are many ways to save information digitally, but they can sometimes be lost in collections you never return to and the connections between them are hard to visualize. Instead, I routinely print articles, rip stories out of magazines and put them into a *single* trend folder which sits on my desk. Saving ideas offline allows me to physically spread them out later to analyze more easily.

✓ **Use a Timer** – If given the chance, most of us will naturally take the time to analyze something that we see or find in a moment. Being fickle is partially about intentionally delaying that process and using a timer can help. The other benefit of literally using a timer when you are consuming some type of new media is that it forces you to evaluate things more quickly on a top level and then leave them behind as you move to something else.

- ✓ **Take Notes with Sharpies** – Many of the articles and stories I find throughout the year are marked with just a few words of notes about the theme of the article and story. I use a Sharpie marker because the thicker lettering stands out and encourages me subtly to write less. This same trick can help you to make only the most useful observations in the moment and save any other ones for later.

## WHAT TO READ

- ✓ *The Laws Of Simplicity* by **John Maeda** – Maeda is a master of design and technology and his advice has guided many companies and entrepreneurs toward building more amazing products. In this exactly 100-page book, he shares some essential advice for learning to see the world like a designer and reduce the noise to see and think more clearly. "More appears like less by simply moving it far, far away," he writes when talking about the power of software as a service or the value of Google. I believe the same principle applies to information and ideas; sometimes you just need distance and time in order to fully appreciate them.

- ✓ *How To Make Sense Of Any Mess: Information Architecture for Everybody* by *Abby Covert* – I have read many books on the art of organizing information, but this is one of my favorites for its smart reasoning and simplified approach. The methods shared in this book by the author (who goes by the pseudonym "Abby the IA") are based on over ten years of teaching methods and worth reading and sharing with your entire team.

## How to Be Thoughtful

In 2014, after 10 years of writing my business and marketing blog, I decided to stop allowing comments. For some readers, this seemed counter to one of the fundamental principles of blogging, which is to create a dialogue. Was it because I thought I was too important to answer comments, or was there something else at work?

The reason I stopped was simple. I had noticed a steady decline in the quality of comments over the 10 years that I had been blogging. What was once a robust discussion that involved thoughtfully worded responses had devolved into a combination of thumbs-up style comments and spam.

Thanks to anonymous commenting and the ease of sharing knee-jerk responses, comments had become *thoughtless* instead of *thoughtful*—and people were starting to notice. So I turned off the comments.

---

**Being thoughtful means taking the time to reflect on a point of view and share it in a considered way.**

---

The web is filled with this type of "conversation." Angry, biased, half thought out responses to articles, people or media. Being thoughful is harder to do when everyone seems to expect thinking to come in real time.

Yet the people who are routinely thoughtful *are* the ones who gain and keep respect. They add value instead of noise...and you can be one of them.

## REAL LIFE ADVICE
## (3 WAYS TO BE MORE THOUGHTFUL TODAY)

✓ **Wait a Moment** – The beauty and challenge of the Internet is that it occurs in real time. We have an idea, and we can share it immediately. It's easy to think that if you can't be the first person to comment on something, that your thoughts are too late. That is rarely true. "Real time" should not mean sharing a comment from the top of your head within seconds. Instead, you should aim to redefine it so your comment is still relevant beyond the particular moment you write it with social media. This means you might choose to take 15 minutes (or longer!) to think about *how* you want to share it.

✓ **Write and then Rewrite** – Anyone who has ever had to write for a long time will tell you that the ultimate way to get better is just to force yourself to do it even if whatever comes out isn't particularly polished. When it comes to being thoughtful with writing, even the most talented writers take the time to rewrite instead of simply sharing the first thing that they write down.

✓ **Embrace the Pauses** – One of the things speakers try to learn as soon as they spend any time standing in front of an audience is how to become comfortable with silence. It's not an easy thing to do. Yet when you can use pauses effectively, you can emphasize the things you really want people to hear or remember. This same principle works whether you are on stage or just engaged in a conversation. The trick is to use those pauses as times to find the right words so you *can* be more thoughtful when you eventually do share your point of view.

## WHAT TO READ

✓ *Brain Pickings* **by Maria Popova** - Popova describes herself as an "interestingness hunter-gatherer" and she writes Brain Pickings, one of the most popular independently run blogs in the world. On the site she publishes articles combining lessons from literature, art and history on wide ranging topics like creative leadership and the gift of friendship. Every year she pores thousands of hours into publishing thoughtful pieces and her readers reward her by donating to support the continued ad-free operation of the site. The way she presents her thoughts is a perfect aspirational example of how to publish something thoughtful week after week – and a model I was inspired to try for myself in my weekly curated email newsletter.

## How to Be Elegant

Jeff Karp is a scientist inspired by elegance … and jellyfish.

As an associate professor at Harvard Medical School, Karp's research focuses on using bio-inspiration—inspiration from nature—to develop new solutions for all types of medical challenges. His self-named Karp Lab has developed innovations such as a device inspired by jellyfish tentacles to capture circulating tumor cells in cancer patients, and better surgical staples inspired by porcupine quills.

Nature is filled with elegant solutions, from the way that forest fires spread the seeds of certain plants to the way termites build porous structures with natural heating and cooling built in.

Ian Glynn, author of the book *Elegance In Science*, argues that elegant proofs or theories have most or all of the following features: they are simple, ingenious, concise and persuasive; they often have an unexpected quality, and they are very satisfying.

I believe it is this idea of simplicity that is fundamental to developing elegant ideas. As Einstein famously said, "make things as simple as possible, but not simpler."

---

**Being elegant means developing your ability to describe a concept in a beautiful and simple way for easy understanding.**

---

A good example of things described beautifully is in what talented poets do. Chances are you don't spend much time with poetry. That is a missed opportunity. Great poetry has simplicity, emotion, and beauty *because* words are taken away. Poets are masters of elegance, obsess over language, and understand that less can mean more.

You don't need to become a poet overnight, but some of these principles can help you get better at creating more elegant descriptions of your own ideas.

For example, think back to the last time you encountered something that was poetically written. It may have been something you once read in school, or perhaps a Dr. Seuss book that you read to a child at bedtime.

Dr. Seuss in particular had a beautiful talent for sharing big ideas with a simplicity and elegance:

- "Today you are you, that is truer than true. There is no one

alive who is youer than you."
- "A person's a person, no matter how small."
- "Everything stinks till it's finished."

We love to read or see elegant stories and we delight in their ability to help us get the big picture with ease, but they do not seem quite so simple to develop or write. If you have ever sat down with paper or in front of a computer screen and tried to tell a simple story you know that it is not an easy challenge.

But we all have the power to simplify our ideas and share them in more elegant ways. To illustrate how, let me take you behind the scenes of the process I used in previous trend reports to name my trends.

## REAL LIFE ADVICE
## (3 WAYS TO THINK MORE ELEGANTLY TODAY)

✓ **Start with the Obvious** – One of my favorite trends from my *2015 Non-Obvious Trend Report* was something I called *Selfie Confidence*. The name was a play on "Self Confidence" and was written to force people to reevaluate something they already knew about and see it in a new light. Selfies are seen as demonstrations of narcissism - but this trend introduced the idea that selfies could actually contribute to helping people grow their self-confidence. The new perspective and unexpected name made this one of the most popular trends from my report that year.

✓ **Keep It Short** – One thing you will notice if you look back on any of my previous trend reports is that most trends are no longer than two words. Elegance often goes hand in hand with simplicity and this usually means using as few words as possible. When it comes to defining and curating ideas, it is perfectly fine to start by describing them with as many words as you need. When you get to the point of trying to add more elegance, though, a necessary component will usually be reducing the words you use to name *and* describe it.

✓ **Use Poetic Principles** – There are some basic principles that poets use when writing that can also be helpful for anyone who is curating trends. One of them is to try and use metaphors and imagery instead of obvious ways of sharing something. Another is to rhyme words or use alliteration to add symmetry to an idea. If you flip to Part II of this book, you will see many places where I used these principles to describe trends like "Preserved Past" or "Lovable Unperfection." A trend from my first report in 2011, Likeonomics, even inspired me to write a book with the same title a year later.

## WHAT TO READ

✓ *Einstein's Dreams* **by Alan Lightman** – Lightman was the first professor at MIT to receive a joint appointment in the sciences and the humanities and is a trained physicist and a poet. His book *Einstein's Dreams* has been one of my favorites for years because of how it imagines what Einstein's dreams must have been like and explores them in a beautiful way through short chapters with interesting assumptions about time and space. This is not a book of poetry, but it will introduce you to the power of poetic writing while also offering the most elegant description of how time might actually work that you'll ever read.

# Why *These* 5 Habits?

Looking back, the fact that I shared these particular habits to help you learn the art of curating ideas may seem a bit random. What makes these five habits stand out? The fact is, the process of how I came to these five was an interesting exercise of curation in itself.

Over the past several years, I read interviews with professional art curators and how they learned their craft. I bought more than a dozen books written by trend forecasters, futurists and innovators. I interviewed dozens of top business leaders and authors. I carefully studied my own behavior, and (as I mentioned earlier in the chapter) I tested the effectiveness and resonance of these habits by teaching them to my students at Georgetown University and to business professionals in private workshops.

Ultimately, I selected the five habits presented in this chapter because they were the most helpful, descriptive, easy to learn and effective once you learn to put them into action.

So as a final recap before we get started with a step-by-step approach to curating trends, let's do a quick review:

## THE 5 HABITS OF TREND CURATORS

1. **Being *curious*** means asking questions about why things work the way they do, and embracing unfamiliar situations or topics with a sense of wonder, and commitment to learning.

2. **Being *observant*** means training yourself to see the details that most others often miss.

3. **Being *fickle*** means capturing ideas without feeling the need to fully understand or analyze them in that moment.

4. **Being *thoughtful*** means taking the time to reflect on a point of view and share it in a considered way.

5. **Being *elegant*** means developing your ability to describe a concept in a beautiful and simple way for easy understanding.

# 5 HABITS OF TREND CURATORS

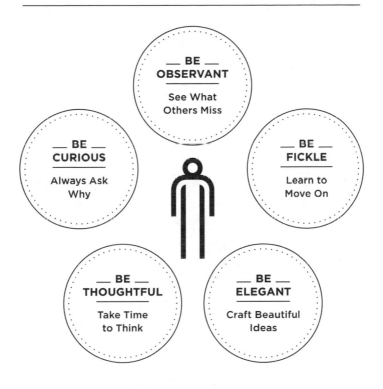

# THE HAYSTACK METHOD:
## How to Curate Trends for Fun and Profit

"THE MOST RELIABLE WAY TO ANTICIPATE THE FUTURE
IS THE UNDERSTAND THE PRESENT."
—JOHN NAISBITT, Futurist and Author of *Megatrends*

In 1982, a single book called *Megatrends* changed the way governments, businesses and people thought about the future.

In the book, author John Naisbitt was one of the first to predict our evolution from an industrial society to an information society, and he did so more than a decade before the Internet. He also predicted the shift from hierarchies to networks and the rise of the global economy.

Despite the book's unapologetic American-style optimism, most of the 10 major shifts described in the book were so far ahead of their time that when it was first released one reviewer glowingly described it as "the next best thing to a crystal ball." With over 14 million copies sold worldwide, it is still the single best-selling book about the future published in the last 40 years.

In the decades since the book came out, Naisbitt has been asked the same question in dozens of interviews with the media: how did he develop his ability to predict the future and could others learn to do it?

For his part, Naisbitt believed deeply in the power of observation to understand the present before trying to predict the future (as the opening quote to this chapter illustrates). In interviews, friends and family often described Naisbitt as having a "boundless curiosity about people, cultures and organizations."

A profile piece in *USA Today* back in 2006 even noted his penchant for scanning "hundreds of newspapers and magazines, from *Scientific American* to *Tricycle*, a Buddhism magazine" as a symbol of his incessant desire to learn.

John Naisbitt was and still is (at the age of 87!) a collector of ideas. His thinking has inspired me for years to think about the world with a similarly broad lens and to develop the process I use for my own trend work: the Haystack Method.

## Inside the Haystack Method

It is tempting to describe the art of finding trends with the cliché of finding a "needle in a haystack." This common visual reference brings to mind the myth of trend spotting that I discounted earlier in this section. Uncovering trends hardly ever involves spotting them sitting neatly inside a so-called stack of "hay" waiting to be discovered.

---

**The Haystack Method describes a process where you first focus on gathering stories and ideas (the hay) and *then* use them to define a trend (the needle) that gives meaning to them all collectively.**

---

In this method, the work comes from assembling the information and curating it into groupings that make sense. The needle is the insight you apply to this collection of information in order to describe what it means—and to curate information and stories into a definable trend.

Trend curators don't seek needles, they gather the hay and then *create* the needle to put into the middle of it.

While that describes the method with metaphors, to truly learn how to do it for yourself, we must go much deeper starting with my personal story of why I created it in the first place.

# THE HAYSTACK METHOD

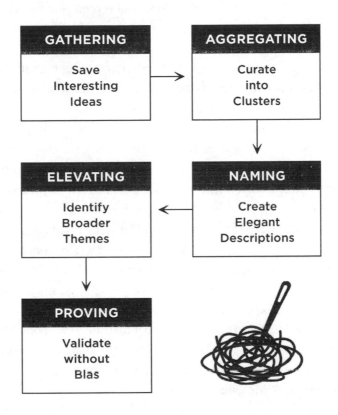

| GATHERING | AGGREGATING |
|---|---|
| Save Interesting Ideas | Curate into Clusters |

| ELEVATING | NAMING |
|---|---|
| Identify Broader Themes | Create Elegant Descriptions |

| PROVING |
|---|
| Validate without Bias |

## Why I Started Curating Ideas

The Haystick Method was born from frustration.

In 2004, I was part of a team that was starting one of the first social media–focused practices within a large marketing agency. The idea was that we would help big companies figure out how to use social media.

Back then "social media" mainly referred to blogging since it was before Facebook and Twitter. The real aim of our team was to help brands work with influential bloggers. There was only one problem with this well-intentioned plan—none of us knew very much about blogging.

So, we all did the only thing that seemed logical to do: each of us started blogging for ourselves.

In June of that year I started my "Influential Marketing Blog" with an aim to write about marketing, public relations and advertising strategy. My first post was on the dull topic of optimal screen size for web designers. Within a few days I ran into my first challenge: I had no plan for what to write about next.

How was I going to keep this hastily created blog current with new ideas and stories when I already had a full time day job that didn't officially involve spending time writing a blog?

I realized I had to become more disciplined about how I collected ideas.

At first my aim was just to find ideas for blog posts, scratched into a notebook or emailed to myself. Then, I included ideas from the many brainstorms I was involved in on a daily basis. Pretty soon I was saving quotes from books, ripping pages out of magazines and generating plenty of blog posts (and client ideas!) based on the ideas I had collected.

These first four years of blogging led to my first book deal with McGraw-Hill. Several years later, the desire to write a blog post about trends based on ideas I had collected across the year led me to publish the first edition of my *Non-Obvious Trend Report* in 2011.

My point in sharing this story is to illustrate how collecting ideas helped me to get better at saving and sharing ideas that people cared about. I became a collector of ideas - which describes perfectly the first step in the Haystack Method.

# Step 1—Gathering

Photo: Curated collection of articles after a year of gathering stories.

**Gathering is the disciplined act of collecting stories and ideas from any interaction you have with people or experiences.**

Do you read the same sources of media religiously every day? Or do you skim Twitter occasionally and sometimes follow the links to continue reading? Regardless of your media consumption, chances are you encounter plenty of interesting stories or ideas. The real question is, do you save them?

The key to gathering ideas is making a *habit* of saving interesting things in a way that allows you to find and explore them later.

My method involves always carrying a small Moleskine notebook in my pocket and keeping a folder on my desk to save media clippings and printouts. By the time you read these words, that folder on my desk has changed color and probably already says "2018 Trends" on the outside of it.

In my process, I start the clock every January and complete it each December for my annual *Non-Obvious Trend Report* (Part II of this book). Thanks to this deliverable, I have a clear starting and ending point for each new round of ideas that I collect.

You don't need to follow as rigid of a calendar timetable, but it is valuable to set yourself a specific time when you can go back and reflect on what you have gathered to uncover the bigger insights (a point we will explore in subsequent steps).

---

### IDEA SOURCES—Where to Gather Ideas

1. Personal conversations at events or meetings (ask lots of questions)

2. Listening to live speakers or TED Talks (write down memorable quotes)

3. Entertainment (TV shows and movies that actually make you think)

4. Books (Nonfiction and fiction)

5. Museums (the more obscure the better!)

6. Magazines and newspapers (as unexpected or outside your realm of knowledge as possible)

7. Travel! (even if it doesn't seem exotic or far away)

---

As you first read this list of sources, they might seem, well, obvious. It is rarely the *sources* of information themselves that will lead you toward a perfectly packaged idea or trend. Rather, mastering the art of gathering valuable ideas means training yourself to uncover interesting ideas across multiple sources and become diligent about collecting them.

## TIPS & TRICKS: HOW TO GATHER IDEAS

- **Start a Folder** – A folder on my desk stores handwritten ideas, articles ripped out of magazines and newspapers, printouts of articles from the Internet, brochures from conferences and just about any other ideas I find interesting. This folder lets me store things in a central and highly visible way. You might choose to create this folder digitally, or with paper. Either way, the important thing is to have a centralized place where you can save ideas for later digestion.

- **Always Summarize** – When you are collecting ideas on a longer time scale, it is easy to forget why it seemed significant in the first place. To help jog your own memory, get into the habit of highlighting a few sentences, or writing down a few notes about your thoughts on the idea. Later, when you are going through your gathered ideas, these notes will be useful in recalling what originally sparked your interest.

- **Seek Concepts, Not Conclusions** – As we learned in Chapter 2, a key habit of good curating is the ability to be fickle. In practice, this means not getting too hung up on the need to quantify or understand every idea you save in the moment. Many times, the best thing you can do is to gather something, save it, and then move on to the rest of your daily life. Perspective comes from taking time and having patience.

## Step 2—Aggregating

Photo: Aggregated stories, sorted into groupings of similar topics or related ideas.

**Aggregating involves taking individual ideas and disconnected thoughts and grouping them together based on bigger themes.**

Once you have been diligently gathering ideas, the next step is to choose a time to go and combine the early results of your observation and curiosity with thoughtful insights about what it means and how it fits together.

When you move from gathering to aggregating, you are taking the first step toward adding bigger insights to stories and ideas. Using a series of questions can help you do that – and here are some of my favorites.

---

### AGGREGATING QUESTIONS—How to Group Ideas

1. What broad group or demographic does this story describe?

2. What is the underlying human need or behavior that this idea is an example of?

3. What makes this story interesting as an example?

4. How is this same phenomenon affecting multiple unrelated industries?

5. What qualities or elements make me interested in this story?

---

At this stage it is important to remember that industries or categories don't matter for grouping. When sorting, don't fall into the "obvious" trap of putting all the financial services examples together or putting every story related to Facebook together.

---

**Aggregating involves sorting ideas based on insights and human motivations, not industries or demographics.**

---

For example, when I was preparing my *2012 Non-Obvious Trend Report*, I collected marketing stories of new campaign strategies from three different companies, Domino's Pizza, Ally Bank (an online consumer bank) and Aviva (world's sixth largest insurance provider). The industries across these examples ranged from banking to food services to insurance.

The shared lesson behind each of their efforts though was h...
companies were finding new ways to avoid being faceless and find their
humanity, so I aggregated them together in a group and wrote on an
index card "companies being more human."

In this second step, it is not important to come up with a fancy name
or even to do extensive research around any stories. Instead, you want to
start building small clusters of ideas which bring together disconnected
concepts into broader groups to be analyzed later.

## TIPS & TRICKS: *HOW TO AGGREGATE IDEAS*

- **Focus on Human Needs** – Sometimes focusing on a bigger
  underlying human emotion can help you see the basis of the
  example and why it matters. For example, the basic human
  need for *belonging* fuels many of the activities people engage
  in online, from posting social comments to joining online
  communities. The more you are able to connect the ideas you
  have gathered with the basic human needs behind them—the
  more easily you can start to aggregate ideas.

- **Recognize the Obvious** – Along the path to uncovering
  "non-obvious" insights, there is some value in recognizing
  and even embracing the obvious. In a grouping exercise for
  example, you can often use the obvious ideas (like multiple
  stories about new wearable technology products) as a way of
  bringing things together and work later on discovering the
  non-obvious insights in between them.

- **Follow Your Intuition** – When you train yourself to be more
  observant, you might also find that you start to develop a
  feeling for stories that somehow *feel* significant or fit together
  even though you may not be able to describe why. Embrace
  that intuition when it tries to surface a connection between
  ideas without the words to describe it. In later phases, you
  can think further about connecting these pieces into a more
  thoughtful trend concept.

# Step 3—Elevating

Photo: Example of how elevating ideas lead to possible trend descriptions.

---

**Elevating means thinking bigger about the underlying themes that connect groups of ideas to describe a single broader concept.**

---

If you have gone through gathering and aggregating ideas—this is the point where you will probably confront the same problem I do every year.

*There are too many possibilities.*

When I go through my annual exercise of curating trends, the first time I aggregate all of my ideas it usually yields between 70 and 100 possible trend topics. That is a sign that there is more work to be done.

So, in this third step, the aim is to take a bigger view and connect groups of ideas together into something that could eventually describe a trend.

1. What interests me most about these ideas?

2. What elements could I have missed earlier?

3. What is below the surface?

4. What is the bigger picture?

5. Where is the connection between ideas?

This can be the most challenging phase of the Haystack Method as combining ideas can also lead you to unintentionally make them too broad (and obvious). Your aim in this step therefore must be *elevating* an idea to make it bigger and more encompassing of multiple examples.

For example, when I was producing my *2014 Non-Obvious Trend Report* I came across an interesting healthcare startup called GoodRx, which had a tool to help people find the best price for medications. It was simple, useful and the perfect example of an evolving shift toward empowering patients in healthcare, which I wrote about in my earlier book *ePatient 2015*.

At the same time, I was seeing retail stores like Macy's investing heavily in creating apps to improve their in-store shopping experience, and a suite of new fashion services like Rent the Runway designed to help people save time and money while shopping.

On the surface, a tool to save on prescriptions, an app for a department store and a crowdsourced tool for renting dresses don't seem to have much in common. I had therefore initially grouped them separately.

While elevating trends, though, I realized that all of them had the underlying intent of helping to *optimize* a shopping experience in some way. I put them together and ultimately called the trend *Shoptimization*, to describe how technology was helping consumers optimize the process of buying everything from fashion to medical prescriptions.

In the next step, we will talk about techniques for naming trends (and the backstory behind the term *Virtual Empathy*), but for now my point in sharing that example is that elevation is the step in the Haystack

Method where you can start to make the connections across industries and ideas that may have initially seemed disconnected and fallen into different groups.

I realize the difference between aggregating ideas and elevating them may seem very slight. In fact, there are times when I manage to do both at the same time because the act of aggregating stories together may help you to broaden your conclusions about them.

In the Haystack Method, I chose to still present these steps separately because most of the time they do end up as distinct efforts. With practice though, you may get better at condensing these two steps together.

## TIPS & TRICKS: *HOW TO ELEVATE AGGREGATED IDEAS*

- **Use Words to Elevate** – When you have groups of ideas, sometimes boiling them down to a couple of words to describe them can help you to see the common themes between them. When I was collecting ideas related to entrepreneurship for my 2014 report, for example, a word that kept emerging was "fast" to describe the growing ecosystem of on-demand services for entrepreneurs. It was the theme of speed that helped me to bring the pieces together to eventually call that trend *Instant Entrepreneurship.*

- **Combine Industry Verticals** – Despite my own cautions against aggregating ideas by industry sector, sometimes a particular trend ends up heavily focused in just one sector. When I see one of these clusters of ideas predominantly focused in one industry, I always try to find another batch of ideas I can combine it with. This often leads to bigger thinking and helps to remove any unintentional industry bias I may have had when first aggregating ideas together.

- **Follow the Money** – With business trends, sometimes the underlying driver of a particular trend is focused on revenue generation for the businesses using it. Following this trail can sometimes lead you to make connections you might not have considered before. This was exactly how studying a new all-you-can-read ebook subscription service and the growth of cloud-based software led me to my 2014 Non-Obvious Trend of *Subscription Commerce*. Both were examples of brands transforming their business models to rely on subscriptions (a trend that has continued to grow in the past year with recent big investments from both Unilever and Proctor & Gamble in subscription businesses).

## Step 4—Naming

**Naming trends involves describing an elevated idea in an easily understandable and memorably branded way.**

Naming trends is a bit like naming a child—you think of every way that the name might unintentionally be dooming your idea (or child) to a life of ridicule and then you try to balance that with a name that feels right.

Of course naming trends also involves the choice of sharing a specific point of view in a way that names for kids generally don't. Great trend names convey meaning with simplicity—and they are memorable.

For that reason, this is often my favorite part of the Haystack Method, but also the most creatively challenging. It is focused on that critical moment when you have the ability to craft an idea that will either stick in people's minds as something new and important or be forgotten.

Sometimes this quest to share non-obvious ideas leads me to invent an entire concept.

My second book which focused on how likeability is the key to success in business is a perfect example of this. It was called *Likeonomics* and focused on exploring why we do business with people we like.

Back in 2006, I published a blog post on how content could be optimized for social media sharing. I called it *Social Media Optimization* and gave it the acronym of SMO. The idea spawned over a dozen services companies still in business today and even has its own entry in Wikipedia.

Finding the right name for an idea can do that. It can help a smart idea to capture the right peoples' imaginations and help them to own and describe it for themselves. Of course, that doesn't make it easy to do.

In fact, naming trends can take just as long as any other aspect of defining or researching a trend. In my method, I try many possibilities. I jot down potential names on post-it notes and compare them side by side. I test them with early readers and clients. Only after doing all of that do I finalize the names for the trends in each of my reports.

---

**NAMING QUESTIONS—**
**How to Ensure You Have an Effective Trend Name?**

1. Is the name not widely used or already well understood?

2. Is it relatively simple to say out loud in conversation?

3. Does it make sense without too much additional explanation?

4. Could you imagine it as the title of a book?

5. Are you using words that are unique and not overused or cliché?

6. Does it build upon a popular theme or topic in an unexpected way?

---

So how do the names turn out? Of course, you could see the list of trends in Part II of this book to compare some of the trend names I developed for this year's report—but here are a few others from previous reports along with a little of the backstory behind the development and selection of each one:

- *Virtual Empathy (2016)* - During a time when virtual reality was all anyone thinking about the future could talk about, the underlying usages that were creating the most emotional connection seemed to have the same thing in common - they amplified our sense of empathy. As a result, I paired the term "Virtual" with "Empathy" instead to create a new way of thinking about the powerful effects of Virtual Reality.

- *Experimedia (2015)* - The pieces for this trend name came together quite quickly as I found a number of articles all talking about how social experiments were creating a new category of media stories. Putting "experiment" together with "media" works because the prefix of "experiment" remains unchanged, while a new ending creates a word that engages people's curiosity while still being clear enough that you could guess the meaning.

- **_Obsessive Productivity_ (2014)** – As the life-hacking movement generated more and more stories of how to make every moment more productive, I started to feel that all of these tools and advice about helping each of us optimize every moment was bordering on an obsession. The naming of this trend was easy, but to me it worked because it combined a word most people associate as negative (obsessive) with a play on one that is usually discussed as a positive (productivity).

While there are literally dozens of ways to name trends, the following tips and tricks share a few of the techniques that I tend to use most often in naming and branding the trends in my reports.

## TIPS & TRICKS: *HOW TO CREATE POWERFUL NAMES*

- **Mashup** – Mashups take two different words or concepts and put them together in a meaningful way. *Likeonomics* is a mashup between likeability and economics. *Shoptimization* is a mashup between shopping and optimization. Using this technique can make an idea immediately memorable and ownable, but can also feel forced and artificial if not done artfully. There is a reason I didn't call my book *Trustonomics*. The best mashups are easy to pronounce and as close to sounding like the original words as possible. Both *Likeonomics* and *Shoptimization* sound like the words they are derived from, which makes them less likely to feel forced or over the top.

- **Alliteration** – When naming brands, this technique is commonly used by brands like Coca-Cola or Krispy Kreme. The idea of using two words beginning with the same consonant is one I have used for trends like *Reverse Retail* or *Disruptive Distribution*. Like mashups, it can feel forced if you put two words together that don't belong, but the technique can lead you toward a great trend name.

- **Twist** – The technique involves taking a common idea or obvious phrase and inserting a small change to make it different. My favorite 2015 example is a trend I called *Small Data*. This was inspired by the growing topic of "big data" and the strategy to use a term that was already commonly used and then giving it a little twist to help it stand out. My "unperfection" trend was similar – just enough of a twist on the actual word "imperfection" to feel new and different.

## Step 5—Proving

**Proving is the final step in ensuring that there are enough examples and concrete research to justify why an idea does indeed describe the accelerating present enough to be called a trend.**

Up until this point in the process of developing and curating trends, you might be thinking there hasn't been much hard data or surveys involved. In the process I have shared so far, that is true.

The Haystack Method relies heavily on analyzing stories and ideas that have been collected over an extended period of time and spotting patterns in those ideas. When it comes to proving a trend idea, though, getting other types of research and data is often the a critical last step.

In part, the amount of data and original research you might require depends on how you are looking at using a trend. The more analytical or scientific your stakeholders and audience, the more likely it is you will need some traditional data to support your curated trends.

Regardless of what type of supporting trend research you intend to use, every trend should have three critical things: idea, impact and acceleration.

## WHAT IS A TREND?

A trend is a unique curated observation
of the accelerating present.

# 3 ELEMENTS OF TRENDS

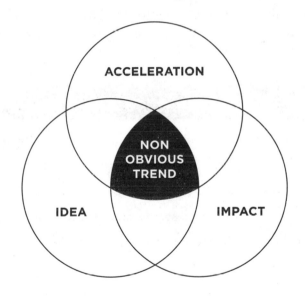

ACCELERATION

NON
OBVIOUS
TREND

IDEA

IMPACT

Let's look at each of these three elements.

1. **Idea** – Great trend ideas are unique descriptions of a shift in culture, business or behavior in a concise enough way to be meaningful without being over simplified.

2. **Impact** – A trend has impact when it causes people to start changing behavior, or companies to adapt what they are selling or how they are selling it.

3. **Acceleration** – The last critical element of great trends is how quickly they are affecting business and consumer behavior and whether that is likely to continue into the future.

For the past six years, these three elements have been the central filter I have used to measure my trend ideas and ensure that I apply the right discipline to making sure they are proven. One element of consistently doing this is asking the same types of questions every year to finalize my annual short list of 15 trends.

---

**PROVING QUESTIONS—How to Quantify a Trend**

1. Is the trend idea unique enough to be described as new or fresh?
2. Has anyone published research related to this trend idea?
3. Is the media starting to uncover examples or focus on it?
4. Are there enough examples across industries to show adoption?
5. Is it likely to continue into the foreseeable future?

---

As you go through these questions, you may notice that some of the trend ideas that you have curated, analyzed, elevated and even created names for may not satisfy all these criteria. Unfortunately, you have now reached the toughest step in the Haystack Method: leaving behind trends that you cannot prove.

Abandoning ideas is brutal—especially after you have become attached to them.

It probably won't help that in this chapter I have already advised you to name them before you prove them—which seems logically wrong. You never name something you're going to leave behind, right?

Well, as true as that may be, the problem is that you often *need* to name the trends before you can access their importance. The process of naming helps you understand what a trend is and how you might prove it. Yet you must force yourself to have discipline.

## TIPS & TRICKS: *HOW TO PROVE YOUR TREND IDEAS*

- **Focus on Diversity** – One of the quickest ways to uncover that a trend idea may not actually be a trend is if you are only able to find examples of it in a single industry, category or situation. For example, I remember several years ago considering the idea of "Short-Form Communication" as a trend because of the rapid growth of Twitter and texting but I couldn't find enough diverse examples to prove the trend beyond social media, so I abandoned it.

- **Watch Your Biases** – Nothing will cloud your judgment more quickly than finding a trend that somehow helps your own industry, product or career. This is a tricky subject because part of the intention of curating your own trends may specifically *be* to support a product or belief. Yet it is also where many of the trends that are oversimplified or just plain wrong come from. Real trends don't have apparent industry biases and are not gratuitously self-serving.

- **Use Authoritative Sources** – When it comes to the examples and research that you find to support a particular trend, the more authoritative sources you can find, the better. What this means in practice is using examples that people may recognize or finding research from reputable organizations or academic institutions. These sources can make the difference between selling your vision or having your audience question your conclusions because they don't believe your sources.

Whether your ideal method for proving trends involves relating them back to fundamental human needs or supporting your ideas with examples of successful businesses and quarterly revenue, there are many ways to prove a trend.

The trends you can predict with the Haystack Method are neither focused solely on consumer behavior, nor on global economies. Instead, this method can help you observe and identify patterns in media, culture, business or any other topic that may have particular relevance for you.

As a final step to help you put the Haystack Method into action, let's go through a step-by-step example of how it was applied, using one of the trends from a previous edition of the *Non-Obvious Trend Report*.

# CASE STUDY:
## How to Curate a Non-Obvious Trend

This section was written simultaneously while curating a trend to help illustrate my process further.

The description below takes you through all five steps of the Haystack Method to gather, aggregate, elevate, name and prove a single trend from the 2015 *Non-Obvious Trend Report,* which I called "Engineered Addiction."

### THE TREND— ENGINEERED ADDICTION

*STEP 1—Gathering*

One of the earliest stories I saved, more than a year before the trend was published, was about Dong Nguyen, the creator of mobile game Flappy Bird, which he suddenly pulled from the iTunes and Android stores after millions of downloads. He worried that the game was becoming too addictive.

His unexpected choice seemed significant—though I wasn't yet sure exactly why—so I saved it. Later that same year, I read a book called *Hooked* about how Silicon Valley product designers could build addictive "habit forming products" that seemed to describe perfectly what Nguyen had unintentionally done (and felt so guilty about)—so I saved that idea as well.

## STEP 2—Aggregating

As I started the process of aggregating ideas together from those I had gathered, I started seeing a pattern in examples that seemed to focus on some type of addictive behavior. The Flappy Bird story was about game design that seemed to lead to addiction. The book *Hooked*, by Nir Eyal, was about product design and using it to create addictive habits in people.

To aggregate these together, I focused on the idea of design and the role that interface design seemed to be playing in creating all these addictive experiences. I stapled these stories together to group them and put an index card on top with the simple description "Addictive Design" to describe what I guessed the trend could be.

## STEP 3—Elevating

When I stepped back to look through my initial list of about 75 possible trends, there were several other trend concepts that seemed to possibly be related to this idea of Addictive Design. One in particular was an education-based trend I had started to track around the use of gamification techniques to aid how people of all ages could learn new skills.

I had used the relatively obvious term "Gamified Learning" on an index card stapled to that article to aggregate a piece about the Khan Academy using badges to inspire learning and a startup called Curious that was making learning addictive by creating bite-sized pieces of learning on interesting topics.

The final piece to add to the puzzle as I was aggregating this trend was a book I had read several months earlier called *Salt Sugar Fat* (by Michael Moss), which had also focused on the idea of addiction, but in the world of food manufacturing. The book exposed how snack foods like Oreos and Cheetos had been created to offer a "bliss point" that mimicked the sensations of addiction in most people. Along with the book, I also had several other articles on that topic saved under the term "Irresistible Food."

Adding the potential trend of Gamified Learning together with Addictive Design and considering the idea of Irresistible Food, I realized that there was an elevated trend that they all might be describing that went beyond popular apps or video games. This bigger trend described how all sorts of experiences and products were created to be intentionally addictive based on more than just design or interfaces.

So I put all the stories for each of these three aggregated concepts together and called the elevated grouping "Ubiquitous Addiction."

### STEP 4—Naming

Now that I had plenty of examples as disparate as food manufacturing and online learning, it was time to find a name that would describe this bigger trend. For some trends, a name I develop during either aggregating or elevating the trends might work for the final trend name. Unfortunately, in this case "Addictive Design" seemed too small and "Gamified Learning" was too obvious and niche. The elevated name I had quickly assigned, "Ubiquitous Addiction," also didn't exactly roll off the tongue.

I needed something better.

The final clue as to what the name of the trend could be came from another interview article I read which featured Eyal. In the article, he was specifically talking about his belief that his role was one which he liked to describe as a "behavioral engineer." This idea of engineering instead of just design immediately seemed far better suited to describing what I felt the trend actually was.

After testing a few versions of using the word "engineering" in the title of the trend, I settled on *Engineered Addiction* as the most descriptive and memorable way to describe this trend and all of its components.

### STEP 5—Proving

The final step was to ensure that this was truly a trend that could be proven through more than stories across multiple industries. In this case, the proof was already done, in large part through the exercise of research because I had uncovered so many dimensions to the trend in different industries across the previous steps.

I still wanted more proof, though, so I started looking for more examples or evidence of intentionally addictive products and experiences that had been "engineered." My research led me quickly to a recently published Harvard Study showing why social media had become so addictive for so many, and then to a book by noted MIT anthropologist Natasha Dow Schüll, who spent more than 15 years doing field research on slot machine design in Las Vegas.

Her book, *Addicted By Design*, exposed the many ways that casinos use the experience and design of slot machines to encourage addictive behavior. Together, these were the final elements of proof that would help tell the story completely.

*Engineered Addiction* made my *2015 Non-Obvious Trend Report*, and ultimately was one of the most talked about trends that year..

## Avoiding Future Babble

Now that we have gone through my method used to build out, describe and prove a trend, using the Haystack Method, there is only one final thing left to do—offer a word of advice against one of the biggest dangers of trend forecasting: sinking into nonsense.

Despite my love of trends and belief that any of us has the ability to learn to see trends—the fact is we live in a world frustrated with predictions, and for good reason.

Economists fail to predict activities that lead to global recessions. Television meteorologists predict rain that never comes. And business trend forecasters are perhaps the worst offenders, sharing glassy-eyed predictions about future industries that seem either glaringly obvious or naively impossible.

---

**At least 50% of pundits seem wrong all the time. It's just hard to tell which 50%.**

---

In 2011 journalist Dan Gardner wrote about this mistake-ridden obsession with the future in his entertainingly insightful book *Future Babble*. Part of his aim was to spotlight the many ways that experts have led us down mistaken paths and caused more harm than good.

In the book, he refers to the research of Philip Tetlock, a psychologist from the University of California's Haas School of Business. Over the span of years, Tetlock and his team interviewed all types of experts and collected 27,450 predictions and ideas about the future. They then analyzed these judgments from their many anonymous sources and concluded that "the simple and disturbing truth is that the experts' predictions were no more accurate than random guesses."

> *No matter how clever we are, no matter how sophisticated our thinking, the brain we use to make predictions is flawed and the world is fundamentally unpredictable.*
>
> Dan Gardner, *Future Babble*

The more interesting conclusion from Tetlock's research, which Gardner highlighted, was the wide disparity in how some experts reacted to the news of hearing their predictions were wrong.

The experts that fared worst were the ones who struggled with uncertainty. They were overconfident, described their mistaken predictions often as being *almost* right and generally had an unchanging worldview. In *Future Babble*, Gardner calls these experts "hedgehogs."

On the other side were experts who did not follow a set path. They were comfortable with being uncertain and accepted that some of their predictions could be wrong. Gardner called these experts "foxes" and described them as modest about their ability to predict the future, self-critical and willing to express doubt about their predictions.

His discussion of foxes versus hedgehogs gets to the heart of an important question that you might be wondering yourself at this point in the book. How do I know with certainty if my predictions are good – and how can you know the same thing about your own?

## The Art of Getting Trends Right (and Wrong)

You already know that I believe anyone can learn to predict the future.

Yet I also shared Dan Gardner's caution about the dangers of false certainty and general skepticism around future predictions for a reason. If you are going to build your ability to curate trends, you also must simultaneously embrace the idea that sometimes you will be wrong.

In Part IV of this book, you will see a summary of previous trends I have predicted along with a corresponding letter grade and a retrospective analysis of its longevity.

Some of them are embarrassingly off the mark.

The reason I share them candidly anyway is partly to illustrate Gardner's point. I want to be as honest with you as I try to be with myself after each year's report. Foxes are comfortable with uncertainty and know they may sometimes be wrong.

I *know* I am sometimes wrong, and I guarantee that you will be, too.

So, why write a book about predicting the trends and go through this entire process if we both might be wrong at the end of it?

A fear of failure is no excuse not to apply your best thinking and explore big ideas. That's the first reason. The second comes to my true purpose in writing this book—which is only *partially* about learning to predict trends, or telling you what my research says the trends that matter are.

Learning to predict the future has an even more valuable side effect: committing to doing it will make you more curious, observant and understanding of the world around you.

It is this mental shift that may ultimately be the greatest benefit of learning to see and curate trends.

Oscar Wilde once wrote that "to expect the unexpected shows a thoroughly modern intellect." *Non-Obvious* is about building this type of modern intellect through seeing the things that others miss, thinking differently and curating ideas describe the accelerating present in new and unique ways.

Now that I have shared the process and techniques I use to do that every year, let's focus on my predictions for the top trends that will be changing how we buy, sell or believe anything in 2017 with the seventh edition of the *Non-Obvious Trend Report*.

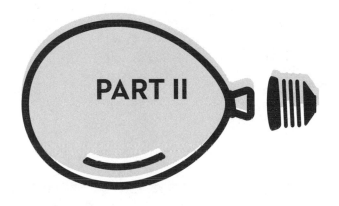

PART II

# THE 2017 NON-OBVIOUS TREND REPORT

# 2017 NON-OBVIOUS TRENDS OVERVIEW – SUMMARY

## WHAT IS A TREND?
*A trend is a unique curated observation about the accelerating present*

**CULTURE & CONSUMER BEHAVIOR** - Trends in how we see ourselves and patterns in popular culture

**Fierce Femininty**

**Side Quirks**

**Desperate Detox**
(Originally Curated 2014)

**MARKETING & SOCIAL MEDIA** - Trends in how brands are trying to influence and engage consumers

**Passive Loyalty**

**Authentic Fameseekers**

**Lovable Unperfection**
(Originally Curated 2014)

**MEDIA & EDUCATION** - Trends in content and information impacting how we learn or are entertained

**Preserved Past**

**Deep Diving**

**Precious Print**
(Originally Curated 2014)

**TECHNOLOGY & DESIGN** - Trends in technology innovation and product design impacting our behavior

**Invisible Technology**

**Robot Renaissance**

**Self-Aware Data**

**ECONOMICS & ENTREPRENEURSHIP** - Trends in business models, startups and careers affecting the future of work or money

**Moonshot Entrepreneurship**

**Outrageous Outsiders**

**Mainstream Mindfulness**
(Originally Curated 2014)

# Chapter 4

# FIERCE FEMININITY

## What's the Non-Obvious Trend?

As our definitions for gender become more fluid, fiercely independent women are increasingly celebrated as heroines, seen as role models and shifting the role of women in modern society.

It is an underappreciated irony of history that modern American women may have the British to thank for their current independence.

In the early 1900s American suffragette Alice Paul visited England and met Emmeline Pankhurst, leader of a group that believed in a more "militant" approach to demanding women's right to vote which involved heckling, window smashing, rock throwing and arson to raise public awareness.

Upon her return to the US, Paul argued that "the militant policy is bringing success. . . the women of England are talking of the time when they will vote, instead of the time when their children would vote."

In 1914, Paul founded her own suffrage organization called the National Woman's Party (NWP) to put these tactics into action.

Over the course of the next several years, her radical tactics got her arrested and imprisoned, where she organized a hunger strike, was forcibly fed, put into solitary confinement and finally created enough sympathy among the public that President Woodrow Wilson eventually ordered her release.

Her lifelong crusade on behalf of women's rights is widely credited with eventually helping women win the right to vote in 1920. What Paul showed the world nearly 100 years ago was that sometimes soft arguments must give way to harsher demands and an unexpected dose of fierceness.

Nearly 100 years later – a new *Fierce Femininity* is taking shape where women are becoming stronger, more independent and capturing power and attention around the world in ways that would have seemed impossible just a decade ago.

Three years ago I featured a trend I called *Powered By Women* aimed at describing the growing role and influence of female leaders in business. Today that trend has evolved more broadly and with a new urgency as women are emerging as heroes who save the day (and the guy) in modern fairy tale stories, and continuing their rise as dominant leaders in business and politics.

Altogether they are reimagining the role of women in modern society – with a strength and fierceness that is surprising.

## The Heroine's Story

Around the same time that I was first writing my 2014 Report, an augmented reality digital comic series titled *Priya's Shakti* was introduced at the Mumbai Comic and Film Convention with an unexpected storyline. It was an immediate viral success despite the taboo backstory of a village girl named Priya who was the survivor of a gang rape and was on a mission to stop violence against women.

The graphic novel was downloaded more than 500,000 times and generated more than 400 stories in the global media. It also brought much needed awareness of sexual violence to a younger generation of Indians.

Priya offers a bold model for a diverse, fierce and strong comic book heroine, but she is only one of many such heroines to emerge from the comics over the past several years.

La Borinquena is a Puerto Rican superheroine who discovers on a family trip to her parent's homeland that she has special powers.

The latest incarnation of long running character "Ms. Marvel" is a 16 year old high school student and Muslim-American girl from New Jersey named Kamala Khan.

Marvel announced that the new "Iron Man" in the comic series will be a 15 year old African American science prodigy and early MIT student named Riri Williams.

This steady shift in comic books to the strong female action hero mirrors a trend in Hollywood. Blockbuster dystopian teen book series like *The Hunger Games* and *Divergent* each feature strong leading women.

The new *Star Wars* film is anchored by a strong female lead character and the Nickelodeon program *Bella and the Bulldogs* features a middle school story where Bella is quarter-back of the football team.

As Jill Soloway, Emmy-winning co-founder of curated online video network Wifey.tv said in a recent interview, "every time I create a show or movie where a woman is a protagonist, we are shifting the way it feels for women to be the center of their stories."

## Play #LikeAGirl

The Cannes Lions award winning campaign from P&G brand Always was launched with the hashtag #likeagirl and sought to reclaim the phrase "like a girl" from being an insult to an empowering idea. The campaign featured a series of videos where girls are challenged to do things like run or throw a ball or fight "like a girl" and brilliantly forced consumers to reevaluate what it means to do anything like a girl.

Global advertising from some of the biggest brands in the world is also making this shift. For example, Under Armour's viral ad featuring African American ballet dancer Misty Copeland and her powerful training regimen has been viewed online more than 10 million times.

Nike has ads in the US featuring the women's soccer team and Nike India recently celebrated fierce, female athleticism in India with its own 2+ minute ad.

This same advertising technique of featuring fierce women is being used by MAC makeup in print ads with Serbian-American competitive body builder and fitness model Jelena Abbou flexing her muscular arms while wearing an evening gown.

Brawny® brand paper towels, a product that has long relied on the masculine image of a lumberjack in a plaid shirt as its icon celebrated Women's History Month this past March 2016, with a new #Strength-HasNoGender campaign that featured the images of four notable women dressed in plaid shirts and looking like suitably fierce female lumberjacks themselves.

As the advertising industry starts to bring in and foster more senior female talent (a growing priority within the industry), this trend toward seeing more powerfully depicted women in marketing and advertising is likely to continue.

## Spinster Power

There is an interesting demographic and cultural side to this trend as well when you consider the growing generation of women who are rejecting the traditional choices of marriage and childrearing for an independent life. In just the past two years, several best-selling books have focused on this shift:

- *All The Single Ladies: Unmarried Women and the Rise of an Independent Nation* (2016) by Rebecca Traister, writer at large for New York magazine and contributing editor at Elle

- *Spinster: Making A Life Of One's Own* (2015) by Kate Bolick, contributing editor at The Atlantic

- *Otherhood: Modern Women Finding A New Kind Of Happiness* (2015) by Melanie Notkin, a startup founder and entrepreneur

When author Kate Bolick was asked about her intentional use of the harsh term "Spinster" to describe these single unmarried women, she said that the word itself "broadcasts our confusion and ambivalence around the single woman."

Journalist Rebecca Traister explored another angle with her acclaimed book *All the Single Ladies* based on more than seven years of research. Traister was inspired by the startling growth of women who were building their adult lives outside the institution of marriage for the first time in recorded history. In just the past generation alone, the median age for first marriages for women went from 22 to 27 – a dramatic shift in a relatively short period of time.

Rather than positioning this as just an indictment of marriage, Traister concluded that these years were creating a new mentality among American women about *whether* they may eventually choose to marry or not. This new generation of women, according to both Traister and Bolick, were perfectly equipped to make the decision for themselves because they are independent minded, better equipped to take care of themselves and less reliant on a male partner for income or security.

These are the new "spinsters" and they count among their ranks some of the most influential women in media and business – from Oprah Winfrey to entrepreneur and former model Tyra Banks. Each has discovered a path to what author Melanie Notkin calls "Otherhood," describing women who either by choice or "circumstantial infertility" don't become mothers – but still find joy and fulfillment in living their lives and being themselves.

## Girl Power in Music

For American recording artist Beyoncé, singing about the power of women is certainly not a new theme. Her single first released in 2008 called "Single Ladies (Put A Ring On It)" has been played as an anthem for women demanding commitment from (mostly) men in films and television for the past decade. In 2011 when she released a new single titled "Run The World (Girls)," it was welcomed by many critics as a more direct and assertive approach to female empowerment.

In 2016, she unexpectedly released her new album Lemonade directly – throwing the music industry into a tailspin of introspection. The album itself is an example of *Fierce Femininity* expressed in a way that only "Queen Bey" (as her fans call her) could deliver.

In the album and companion film, Beyoncé tells the story of her husband cheating on her, going through a range of emotions (intuition, denial, anger, apathy, emptiness, accountability, reformation, forgiveness, resurrection, hope, redemption) and coming through the other side. The album is authentic, unfiltered and powerful – but it is not the only example of the *Fierce Femininity* trend coming to life through music.

Playlists of "girl power" songs are commonly created and shared – with tracks like "Can't Hold Us Down (Christina Aguilera), "Bad Girls" (M.I.A.), "Brave" (Sara Bareilles), "Fight Song" (Rachel Platten) and dozens of others.

Outside of pop music, another example of this type of Fierce Femininity is Vancouver-based artist Jasleen Powar merges her background in slam poetry with an authentic style that includes sampling 90s hits and commonly referencing her Sikh-South Asian heritage. One single from her latest EP titled *Bollywoes* called "Queen" starts with asking the question "what good is a king without a queen?"

It's the perfect question to bring this trend to life.

## Investing In Girls

Professor Rafia Ghubash wants to correct some of the misperceptions about women in the Middle East.

As founder of the Dubai Women's Museum, she appears frequently at global conferences and in media interviews speaking optimistically about the role of women in Dubai, and more broadly in the Middle East. "The media do not promote the achievements of women," she said in one recent interview. "Come to Dubai and UAE and it is wholly apparent that women have equal opportunities and are considered to be equal to men."

Perhaps the most visible promoter of this point of view from the region is the popular Jordanian Queen Rania – who has long been an advocate of women's rights. She is an international icon and has tirelessly used technology to dispel Western myths about the Middle East. Videos from her YouTube channel have been viewed over 14 million times, and she is followed by more than 5 million people on Twitter.

After being named Glamour's Woman of the Year, she told the

magazine, "Look at any country that's plagued with poverty, disease or violence; The antidote is girls. Girls are the antibodies to many of society's ills." In the time since, that message has been brought to life by many other global initiatives – including a popular grassroots movement fueled by the *Girl Rising* documentary film.

First released in 2014, the Girl Rising film from Academy Award-nominated director Richard E. Robbins follows the global stories of nine ordinary girls who confront impossible challenges to pursue their dreams. Since its launch the film has sparked a global conversation about the importance of educating girls that now incorporates public screenings, full teaching curriculums, extended global editions for various regions and community gatherings around the world.

Most importantly, along with physical places like the Dubai Women's Museum and the celebrity power of Queen Rania, the film is a symbol of hope and change for women and girls around the world to see themselves as more liberated, powerful and empowered than ever before.

## Why It Matters:

For years the ideal woman was usually described as someone who could "have it all," be a wife and mom and boss and balance the perfect life of work, home and everything in between. Women were celebrated for being the jugglers in chief of the household and an impossible ideal was created.

Now that façade is breaking and taking its place is a far stronger, more human and more identifiable portrait of womanhood. Women can be fierce, strong, unapologetic. The lines are blurring and standing in the middle is a new generation of women who have control to make the lives they want.

This means more women are choosing to remain single for longer, more women around the world are getting educated and starting companies, more investors are backing women – and perhaps most importantly that more girls around the world are seeing these non-obvious examples and being encouraged to dream about the future for themselves.

## How To Use This Trend:

✓ **Empower female mentors** - Mars Chocolate North America President Tracey Massey spends as much of her time mentoring as she can - and speaks often about its value. Having senior women leaders mentor younger ones is a necessity if the new generation is going to succeed with more confidence and be given more opportunities. And if you happen to be a female leader, consider taking more of your time to be a mentor.

✓ **Think like a woman** - Rather than simply equating men and women as equal, there are a range of books like *The Athena Doctrine, Lean In* and most recently, *Feminist Fight Club* which all offer useful insights on how to balance life and work, succeed in your career and do it with unique femininity. Most interestingly, each of these books is equally valid and insightful even if you happen to be male.

# Chapter 5

# SIDE QUIRKS

---•---

## *What's the Non-Obvious Trend?*

As the global shift toward individualism continues, people of all
ages embrace what makes them unique, follow their passion,
often start a side business and increasingly appreciate
the quirky differences in one another.

A coffee mug is a nearly universal symbol of individuality.

This simple insight is one that the team at online arts and crafts marketplace Etsy uncovered as they prepared in late 2016 to launch their first global brand advertising campaign. The campaign introduced the tagline "Difference Makes Us" and featured an assortment of unique and quirky products (like coffee mugs) which are sold directly to consumers by artistic enthusiasts.

Describing the vision behind the campaign, Etsy CCO Paul Caiozzo said "an important part of this message is: Did you know that something as simple as a coffee cup can reflect what creativity means to you? And on Etsy, there are 200,000 different coffee cups—new, old, antique, used, vintage—that you can get."

The site is most popular among consumers who want a unique hand-crafted gift or product and there is plenty of global demand.

Etsy has more than 25 million buying and selling members – and the marketplace usually has close to 40 million items for sale at any one moment, serving buyers and sellers in nearly 200 countries.

Etsy is the ultimate place for anyone to explore their *Side Quirks* – and provides the perfect introduction to this trend. Not only can consumers find the ultimate product to express their individuality, but aspirational entrepreneurs can realize their dreams by expressing their creativity and making money from their passion.

The quest to buy and sell products not available anywhere else has propelled the growth of the site for more than ten years, but the real secret of the site's success might be because of a global shift that has been decades in the making.

## Rise of Individualism

Social scientists describe the societies of the world as holding two seem-ingly opposite worldviews. "Collectivist" societies value family and group goals over the needs of the individual. In Collectivist cultures like India, China, Korea, Mexico, Japan and most of Africa, the "rules" of society promote working with others, selflessness, and caring for larger extended families.

"Individualistic" cultures, like the USA, Australia, South Africa and most of Europe generally celebrate individual achievement and encour-age people to rely on themselves and focus on their immediate families.

Though those classifications have long been accepted as fact, recently researchers have started to test these assumptions.

For example, one team from the Department of Psychology at the University of Waterloo and Arizona State University led by Professor Igor Grossmann is studying indicators that are commonly associated with individualistic cultures, such as the prevalence of unique baby names, or the percentage of single child or two child families (where kids generally expect and receive more attention than in larger families). Each of these is considered to be a small piece of evidence supporting the conclusion that individualism has been slowly expanding globally over the past 150 years.

The ground-breaking World Values Survey (WVS) has measured people's values and beliefs across the world since 1981. One of the architects of the survey, social scientist Ron Inglehart, has said that the mission of the WVS is to measure everything from support for gender equality to attitudes toward the family, national identity and culture.

One of the key findings from the survey over the past two decades was a rising prevalence of individualism globally - a shift that is commonly referenced in global brand advertising for everything from cars to mobile devices.

Perhaps the most interesting part of this conclusion is how exactly it has been shaping attitudes over the past decade to encourage positive and negative *Side Quirks* in cultures where you would least expect either to thrive...like across Asia.

## Korean Honja, Japanese Hikikomori & Chinese Individualism

When thinking about *Side Quirks*, it is easy to focus on the positive. Individualistic societies tend to celebrate the success of the individual and the quirk that leads them to success. When you consider the example of Asia, individualism is evolving in very different ways than in the West.

Sometimes, the path is not quite so optimistic or empowering. As case in point, let's consider the curious example of the hikikomori in Japan.

The term *hikikomori* is used in Japan to define a reclusive subgenre of (mostly) men who haven't left their homes or interacted with others for at least six months. According to a recent Japanese cabinet survey, there are currently 541,000 young Japanese aged 15 to 39 who could be described as *hikikomori*.

Some have been driven to their solitary existences by failing to live up to societal or parental expectations. Others retreat after being unable to cope with some big conflict. Many end up staying at home with enabling parents who take care of necessities like food and rent.

Part of what makes this type of existence appealing is the easy access to the Internet and technology which allows *hikikomori* to retreat into the digital world. Shifting to the culture in China, technology plays a similarly enabling role – usually without the same debilitating social isolation.

When former J. Walter Thompson Asia-Pacific CEO and longtime Shanghai resident Tom Doctoroff was interviewed by Asia Society, about the state of individualism in China – he had this to say:

> *Young people in China use the internet as much more of an emotional engagement with their own identity. They feel they have opportunities to express themselves in ways that they never could in the real world. So they want to liberate who they are or who they aspire to be in a safe way without coloring outside of the lines. That's why the internet is so powerful for Chinese — because it's virtual and it's relatively anonymous and safe.*

In China, the path for rising individualism goes through the internet. One example of this is the Chinese video-based network YY which features (among other things) gaming videos and karaoke competitions. In South Korea, it is coming from the rising comfort of people are finding "alone time," according to one recent survey.

In late 2016 a well-known Korean jobs portal called Saramin asked 1,593 male and female users aged 20 to 30 years old about their preferences and habits. When asked whether the spread of "individualistic culture" and wanting to enjoy more "me-time" was a positive thing, 86% responded yes. In a culture where going out alone was once considered the behavior of a social outcast (*wangda*), a new vocabulary has emerged in recent years to describe a slew of activities that used to be taboo in Korean culture.

On a recent visit to Asia, a Korean colleague of mine shared that *honbap* is the Korean word for eating alone, *honsul* for drinking alone, and *honyeong* for going to the movies alone. "Hon" is the first syllable from the word *honja* (which means to do something alone in Korean) and an online search for "hon" activities now yields hundreds of results.

In the survey, a majority of respondents felt that technology and social media (often described as "selfie culture" which I explored in my

2016 trend *Selfie Confidence*) had enabled more independent thinking and less desire to conform among Korea's youth.

What can the Japanese *hikikomori*, Korean *honja,* and the way Chinese citizens find and explore their identities online tell us about the power of *Side Quirks*? In some cultures, the quirk may not be exploring a hobby for pleasure – but rather finding yourself through the process of crafting your own personal story and identity online.

In other cases, that quirk might actually lead you to building a profitable side business...which has rapidly become a movement all on its own.

## Side Hustle

When describing a side hustle, it is usually considered as something cash strapped Millennials do for extra spending money. This is an oversimplification that is best dissected in an article by freelance writer Catherine Baab-Muguira.

Her article defines a side hustle in this way:

*Millennials didn't invent the second job, they just branded it. The side hustle offers something worth much more than money: A hedge against feeling stuck and dull and cheated by life. This psychological benefit is the real reason for the Millennial obsession.*

*...in the best-case scenario, your side hustle can be like a lottery ticket, offering the possibility–however remote–that you just might hit the jackpot and discover that holy grail of gigs. The one that perfectly blends money and love. The one that's coming along any day now.*

Baked into this description is a sense of hope and optimism for the future fueled by the side hustle. It offers a purpose that work often does not – and does it in a way that has the potential to lead toward a more desirable career path.

Engaging in your side hustle doesn't always mean you need to quit your day job either. My business partner and friend Paresh Shah is working on an upcoming book right now called *Lifters* which explores the idea of reconciling having a day job with simultaneously exploring your passion and being a force of inspiration to those around you.

Whether you use it inside the company or as an entreprenuer, the side hustle is an example of how *Side Quirk* is affecting careers, how companies attract and retain employees, and the way that we think about work – even for people who are far older than Millennials. The AARP has a frequent stream of articles and advice for people over 50 years old on how to make money on the side while exploring their more artistic passions – from graphic design to saddle making.

As part of last year's trend of *Optimistic Aging* I also wrote about the growing desire for those over 50 to not only remain active in their retirement, but to do so by starting a second career or entrepreneurial venture that they run on the side while enjoying family, travel and more free time than they ever had during their past working years.

*Side Quirks* also go far beyond just turning hobbies into business opportunities. It can also help to humanize leaders who need to better connect with employees and stakeholders.

## Quirky Leadership

At the Coca-Cola shareholder meetings in 2015, billionaire Warren Buffett joked that he probably had enough money to actually buy the world a Coke – referencing the brand's famous jingle from the 1970s. During the meeting the company's biggest single shareholder then went on to take the stage and play a rendition of the jingle on his ukulele.

The performance offered another side of the world's richest man who is often profiled for his investment savvy and charity but rarely for anything else. Playing the ukulele on stage made him seem just a bit more approachable and human. *Side Quirks* can do that in a unique way for any leader.

Most of us have these special types of skills or personal hobbies – but there was a time when they were mainly hidden from few. Job applicants were encouraged not to get too personal on their resume. Executives led more guarded lives away from the public eye and tended to keep their private passions disguised or rarely seen.

That time has changed.

Today more and more leaders are actively sharing their *Side Quirks* with pride as a way to better relate to their employees and community, lead with authenticity and create more personal connections.

It is something I routinely do with stage audiences and clients as well. Anyone who has worked with me or read my bio probably knows that I hate cauliflower, play the drums and buy far more luggage than I could actually use just because I love it. I even have an entire page on my website (linked in the bottom footer) about my well-documented "cauliphobia" as I have sometimes jokingly called it.

Those are my own side quirks, but there are plenty of other leaders who actively share their own any chance they get. Here are a few examples:

- Current Chairman of Alibaba Jack Ma collects crickets and loves to sing at corporate events (a fact that has been regularly captured on video and posted online)
- Former Twitter CEO Dick Costolo is well known for his hobby of beekeeping and often brought fresh honey to the office.
- Adventure CEO Richard Branson has done everything from riding in a hot air balloon to nearly killing himself when speeding down a mountain on a bike.
- Cisco Systems cofounder Sandy Lerner is a big fan of the medieval sport of jousting. She owns lances, costumes, and raises horses for competition.

What all of these CEOs are illustrating is that it now acceptable and even desirable for leaders to show their interests and personality. In fact, it may be a critical component of helping them to connect with their employees.

## Twee Revolution and Generation Z

The final piece of this trend comes from a growing shift in how we define identity and gender. This is mainly driven by the rise of the successors to the millennial generation who are just now entering their teenage years: Generation Z.

In his book *Twee: The Gentle Revolution In Music, Books, Television, Fashion, and Film*, former Spin magazine writer Marc Spitz defines being "Twee" as "the utter dispensing with of 'cool' as it's conveniently known, often in favor of a kind of fetishization of the nerd, the geek, the dork, the virgin."

This new generation (currently aged between 5 to 19 years old) differs from their Millennial siblings in a few important ways. Most notably, according to a research report from marketing agency Sparks & Honey, they have global social circles, are concerned and aware of the world, and far more likely to come from blended cultural backgrounds.

This mixed background creates a curious duality where they want to fit into the group and feel connected, but also have some small quirks can help you use your personality to stand out. These *Side Quirks* are small nuances in how any of us describe ourselves or see our own self-identity.

In some cases this sense comes from uniquely defining gender in unexpected ways which even led Facebook a few years ago to offer 71 standard gender options for people to identify as – along with an open fill-in-the-blank for those who describe themselves as something not yet listed.

In other cases, it can be driven by a shift in how Millennials use a product that has been around for decades. According to research from the NPD group, sales of so-called artisanal fragrances rose 22 percent last year, making them the fastest growing segment in the fragrances industry. A major driver of this sales boom are millennials who, unlike their parents or grandparents, don't want to wear the same scent every day. As one shopper who was interviewed about her fragrance choices by BusinessWeek said: "I don't want to smell like everyone else now. I like to discover new names and buy from small boutiques."

## Why It Matters:

There used to be a global divide between cultures that celebrated individualism and those that did not. Among the ones that did, people were encouraged to find success as an individual but not necessarily encouraged to celebrate the quirks of their personality that make them feel unique and special. These passions and behaviors were once derogatively described as quirks. Now quirks have a new positive meaning and more people are finding joy in embracing these elements of their personality.

In some cases, *Side Quirks* are leading people to start the businesses or volunteer for the causes they always wanted to start or engage with. In other situations, they are just leading people to feel more independent and comfortable spending time alone without the necessity to have others around. While some cultures will continue to struggle with this shift, leaving behind troubled groups like the Japanese *hikikomori*... the vast majority of the impact from this trend will lead to more consumer empowerment, greater self-esteem and the flexibility and freedom to leave a soul-diminishing career for something better.

## How To Use This Trend:

✓ **Celebrate achievements** – One of the hallmarks of this trend is that people like and expect to have successes celebrated in a meaningful way. This means, depending on the culture, you should be ready to make an announcement to honor employees who do well, or encourage teams to take pride in their achievements in a personal way (without the announcement).

✓ **Show your quirks to connect** – When leaders want to build trust, they are often best served by showing some vulnerability. Showing your quirks can be a great way to connect. This might mean sharing a hobby or having a side interest that becomes a reason to connect. Either way, Side Quirks can give people a reason to believe in and trust you more deeply.

✓ **Stand for something** – Inherent in the idea of showing your quirks is being willing to take a stand on behalf of what you think. This is a powerful strategy for brands to stand out and one that you will routinely see beloved brands do. Side Quirks are not just to be embraced in people, but can also bring a brand to life and create more human and emotional connections with customers.

# Chapter 6

# DESPERATE DETOX

## What's the Non-Obvious Trend?

**As technology, media clutter and physical things increase the complexity of our daily lives, people are desperately seeking new ways to enjoy more moments of reflection by simplifying.**

The first time I wrote about *Desperate Detox*, it was all about trying to find a way to escape the irresistible allure of the small screen. As our smartphones dominated hours of every day and the continual beeps and chimes of social media alerts invaded every waking moment – it seemed as though technology was to blame.

Three years have passed since then and we are still as accosted by the beeps and chimes of technology as we ever were … but this trend is no longer about humans versus technology. In 2017, the reason I chose to feature *Desperate Detox* as an annual selection once more is because it has come to describe a broader rejection of complexity instead of simply a rejection of technology.

In an interesting twist to the trend, technology itself has started to offer supportive tools to help provide that much needed "detox" from complexity in all forms.

Perhaps nowhere is this more prevalent than in a growing range of tools that allow us to optimize our lives by slowing down, blocking out or otherwise adapting the things we spend our time on.

## Detox By Slowing Down

In Norway, a popular public television series called "slow TV" has depicted journeys such as a cruise ship's 134 hour journey up the country's west coast, an 7 hour video of a knitting circle – and its most popular (and ridiculed) show – "National Firewood Night," a 12 hour broadcast which features logs being cut and then burned in a fireplace. The channel was such a cult hit that Netflix recently picked it up to syndicate to customers outside of Norway.

In Spain, a curious initiative called "Eating Without Noise" is an effort to fight back against the "café effect" – where restaurants get louder due to the combination of loud conversation and service. So far more than 20 restaurants across the country have declared their intentions to be "quiet dining" venues, including several Michelin-starred restaurants such as Hotel Unico in Madrid. To be on the list, an establishment agrees to maintain a certain minimum distance between tables, add proper sound insulation and encourage diners not to be so noisy when enjoying meals.

The point behind both of these is that there is another path to *Desperate Detox* which on the surface seems to contradict Jeff Kuo's speed watching tactics for television. How can slow TV and fast TV coexist as part of the same trend?

The idea of *Desperate Detox* at its core is about people seeking more simplicity and less clutter in their lives. Some find it by minimizing the time they spend watching television. Others find it through the therapeutic calm of watching a log burn on the television for hours.

## Digital Detox And Travel

In June of 2016, Intel Security (makers of the McAfee Security Software) released the results of a global survey they had conducted asking travelers just how often they were able to resist the temptation of their devices and just choose to enjoy a travel experience without the interference of technology.

The numbers were discouraging.

Canadians were the most successful at staying away from social media use (61 percent) while on vacation. Coming in a close second were the French (60 per cent), followed by Mexicans (54 percent), Germans (54 percent), Americans (53 percent), Dutch (51 percent), Brazilians (51 percent), Spaniards (44 per cent) and Singaporeans (42 per cent).

The survey went on to note that despite the "winning" performance by Canadians, more than half (54 per cent) of Canadian participants who intended to unplug from their digital devices on vacation were still unable to do so … even despite three-quarters of participants saying their vacation was more enjoyable after they unplugged their smartphones and tablets.

So if vacations would be more enjoyable by unplugging, and most of us (like the Canadians) have a hard time *choosing* to do so intentionally – what do we do? Several tour operator have launched recent initiatives to help you find an answer to that question.

For example, pioneering travel tour operator Intrepid Travel launched a series of "Digital Detox" tours of the world, promising "exclusive departures where there'll be no social media, no phones and no cameras. For real. This is travel like it used to be."

There are others creating similar experiences. Discover Outdoors runs tech-free canoe camping adventurous and Paragon Guides brings people out to do llama trekking. Via Yoga runs a series of themed getaways and Wanderlust holds day long festivals on mindful living.

All of this innovation in the travel industry is aimed at helping people use their time when traveling to truly rest and recharge – detoxing their bodies and their minds without the interruption of technology.

## Ownership Is Overrated

Having a great detox moment when you travel can be therapeutic, but it's unlikely to last if you return to a clutter filled home. Over the past year, one best-selling book has been credited with single handedly starting a "decluttering" trend of its own. The book is called *The Life Changing Magic Of Tidying Up* and it is authored by a Japanese professional organizer named Marie Kondo. The book offers a series of tips for decluttering one's life – including how to reorganize closets, throw out things you don't really need and conquer your unreasonable emotional attachment to "stuff."

The book sparked a movement and fit perfectly into a macro trend that has received far more attention – the growth of the "sharing economy." This term is frequently used to describe the rapid growth of platforms and services like Uber and AirBNB which are causing people around the world to rethink their traditional notions of ownership.

According to a survey from Harris Poll, 78% of millennials—compared to 59% of baby boomers—"would rather pay for an experience than material goods." The research supports their belief that experiences are more worthwhile. In his book *Happy Money*, Harvard marketing professor and social scientist Michael Norton suggests that for most people spending money on experiences rather than possessions creates far more happiness.

This shifting belief along with the fact that the collaborative economy allows for more sharing and less owning in many situations means that a growing method for reducing complexity and enjoying a successful *Desperate Detox* is indeed finding a way to acquire less stuff.

## Tech-Enabled Detoxing

At this point it might be tempting to assume that "Desperate Detox" is a trend mainly focused on trying to get rid of clutter or to optimize and slow things down. The flip side that adds a bit of nuance to this trend is considering how many ways people are finding to create moments of detox by strategically *speeding up instead of slowing down*.

In the middle of 2016, reporter Jeff Guo published an article in the *Washington Post* that horrified film makers and content creators around the world. The article delved into a curious habit he had developed to save time – watching television and movies at two times their normal speed.

Using custom software he would accelerate his viewing, allowing him to stream an entire season of a show in a matter of hours. It was his extreme but understandable response to the explosion of scripted and unscripted entertainment that is now available at the click of a button. More than 400 scripted shows were released by American production teams in 2015 – nearly double the number in 2009.

On top of all that, streaming services like Netflix, Hulu, Amazon Prime and YouTube's new RED offer hours more entertainment available whenever you have an idle moment to spare.

Yet the obvious question you might wonder after reading about this curious habit is how anyone could prefer this in the first place. Wouldn't watching a show at an accelerated speed result in chipmunk-like voices and an awful viewing experience?

To let people answer that question themselves, the *Washington Post* also published a sample video clip alongside Guo's contentious article where readers could actually watch a short segment of popular drama *Game of Thrones* in regular speed and at an accelerated speed.

For most people who watched the sample, the accelerated watching experience was undeniably better.

Dialogue came faster, pauses were shortened, and when you returned to watching it at the "normal" speed – everything just seemed to be moving in frustratingly slow motion. Despite the protests of the creators and their desire to keep the artistic integrity intact – the article convincingly encouraged people to discover and adopt this time hack for themselves.

Accelerating video is not the only example over the past year of how technology is helping to offer "detox" from complexity either. A company called Circle recently partnered with Disney to offer a $99 device that watches children's activity online and manages time limits for how long kids are allowed to use devices. Once a limit is reached, access can be switched off.

Going one step further, earlier this year an NYU student named Chino Kim developed a pair of glasses called "Screeners" that immediately turn opaque when they detect that the wearer is viewing a mobile device screen to discourage device time.

What all these efforts have in common is their focus on helping people to "detox" from the noise created by technology and media by using technology itself to solve the problem. Sometimes, though, the best way to silence the technology is to find moments where people might elect to remove it completely.

## Why It Matters:

The complexity of life today from a combination of "always-on" technology to exponentially more demands on our time and attention continues to drive a need among people to find new ways to escape the chaos.

The need for *Desperate Detox* is one that most of us can immediately empathize and recall a moment or two when we wished for this ourselves. Yet the most interesting evolution of this idea is that it no longer is simply about escaping technology. Complexity rather than technology is the enemy, and is increasingly being solved by products, ideas and life-hacks that allow each of us to find more moments of tranquility and more ways to save our own time, or at least spend it in more fruitful ways to increase our own happiness.

## How To Use This Trend:

✓ **Create more mute buttons** - What happens when you email a customer too frequently? They unsubscribe. What if instead of letting them leave, you gave them a way to turn on a mute button for a period of time – or at least turn down the volume a bit? The best marketers know there is a forgotten third option besides letting people opt out or opt in. You can let them *opt for less*. In doing this, you give people a way to reduce the noise without leaving altogether – and the same technique works for situations far beyond email.

✓ **Simplify without dumbing down** - Simplicity has long been an ideal in communications, but sometimes it can also cause you to accidentally dumb down a message or experience and make it meaningless. In the future, communicators of any message and creators alike will need to consider how their experiences can be set up to offer something simpler, while still maintaining the essence of what made it great in the first place. This will take great communication skills, powerful writing, and a significant amount of creative thinking as well.

✓ **Detox your customer experience** – One of the biggest trends in retail is a shift from promotion to experiences, and the best are ones where customers delight in the chance to leave the outside world behind and engage more deeply with a brand. Doing so requires a disciplined process to remove complexity in everything from salesperson interactions to crowded endcap displays, while making sure that the use of technology like augmented or virtual reality is strategic and never gratuitous.

# Chapter 7

# PASSIVE LOYALTY

## *What's the Non-Obvious Trend?*

**As switching from brand to brand becomes easier and technology empowers consumers – a new understanding of loyalty challenges brands to get smarter about earning true loyalty.**

What if all loyal customers aren't as loyal as they seem?

The way most companies think about customer loyalty is singular: you are either a loyal customer or you are not. In recent years, this bias has become apparent through both the rapid growth of investment in loyalty programs and their often disappointing results.

The latest edition of a biennial report from leading loyalty marketing research provider Colloquy found that even though memberships in customer loyalty programs increased by 26% in the US to over 3.3 billion, the typical American household has memberships in 29 loyalty programs but is only active in 12.

When industry consulting firm Maritz Motivation Solutions published its own LoyaltyNext® Customer Study in early 2016, the study found that "43% of consumers join loyalty programs because of the desire to earn rewards. Only 17% of those in loyalty programs say they joined out of love for the brand's products and just 5% because of a shared identity with brand values."

Where most of these programs miss the mark is that they fail to account for the fact that there are two forms of loyalty – the loyalty of convenience (passive) and loyalty of belief (active).

It turns out distinguishing between them can make the difference between greater retention and lifetime customer value.

## How To Distinguish Passive From Active Loyalty

The market for selling automotive insurance is a perfect example of this. On the surface, brands in this space seem to have a loyal base of consumers who renew every year, yet as a recent industry report from consulting firm McKinsey shared, there was "a significant number of customers who are loyal in name only...they remain with their carrier more out of inertia than satisfaction." When seen in this light, the ever present advertising from brands like GEICO and Progressive encouraging and trying to make it easy for consumers to switch makes far more sense.

As the Mckinsey piece noted, "they are giving consumers reasons to leave, not excuses to stay," which also happens to describe the problem of loyalty. While companies are investing more and more effort in trying to entice customers to be loyal – most of the so-called loyalty they are generating is loyalty of convenience.

Another example of the same effect is the commonplace switching behavior among mobile phone consumers, both for their plans and the devices themselves. To accommodate this, Apple has a "Switch to iOS" app in the Google Play store, and Google has created its own "quick switch adapter" to move iPhone content to an Android phone with three simple buttons. Both sides anticipate more than a million "switchers" to leave one platform for the other in the coming year.

Nearly every industry from cable companies to credit cards and mortgage loans have created easy processes to reduce the costs of switching from one to another. The friction and cost of switching used to be far higher. Today, it happens at the push of a button – with a fully automated process behind it to make it seamless to defect and harder to earn active loyalty.

| Passive Loyalty | Active Loyalty |
|---|---|
| ✓ Effortless to sign up or switch | ✓ Alignment with Brand Values |
| ✓ Motivated by signup savings and benefit | ✓ Product/Service affinity |
| | ✓ Promote brand as ambassador |
| ✓ Focused on Rewards | ✓ Drives referrals (Net Promoter) |
| ✓ Convenience drives loyalty | ✓ Values Rewards |
| ✓ No major affinity, referrals or proactive engagement with company | ✓ May go out of way for loyalty |
| | ✓ Not prone to switch (even for upfront incentive) |

Customers chase better deals, look to save money and reward businesses who give them those things in the short term – but will eventually move on, leave and give their short term loyalty to another brand, until they repeat the same cycle.

One early research study on the nature of passive vs. active loyalty dubbed this phenomenon as a consumers "state of inertia" and concluded that "a passively loyal consumer might buy the same brand for 5 or 6 time periods out of inertia ('lock-in'), but after that she is likely to include other brands in her consideration set."

So how can any group or leader create more *actively* loyal consumers, followers or employees?

Just three years ago, it seemed like subscriptions might be the answer.

## The Rise And Fall Of The Subscription Economy

Many industry analysts who closely track the evolution of ecommerce and business were projecting that the "subscription economy" was going to change the world. You could "subscribe" to razor blades (Dollar Shave Club) or weekly meal plans (Blue Apron) or even software like Adobe

Photoshop and Microsoft Office. Everywhere you turned the idea of access trumping ownership was inspiring businesses to try and create a subscription out of everything.

Why sell a product once when you could sell a subscription to generate revenue every month?

The dramatic growth of this industry led me to include *Subscription Commerce* as one of my Economics & Entrepreneurship trends in 2014. A key example I used at the time was the early rise of subscription boxes – curated packed boxes with multiple products arranged around a theme.

Led by pioneering beauty box brand Birchbox in 2011, the subscription commerce industry as a whole was growing at 200% a year and generating over $5 billion in revenue.

Then it seemed to hit a wall. The low barriers to entry and high cost of acquiring subscribers in the first place started to affect the market. Competition intensified and growth began to stall.

In 2016, Birchbox conducted two rounds of layoffs and shifted their strategy to include more retail product sales online and a bricks-and-mortar store. Meanwhile, men's fashion subscription commerce retailer Trunk Club closed its distribution center in Chicago and integrated more operations with parent company Nordstrom.

Tech publication recode.com dubbed it the "end of gimmick commerce" and it seemed we had moved past the subscription commerce fad. Yet the underlying consumer behavior behind its rise remained unchanged. Consumers still want convenience above all else. While the popularity of subscriptions boxes started to wane, the power of the business model behind them has not. For proof, consider the latest innovation from the Internet's biggest retailer and its plan for how it will leverage them.

## Automated Consumerism

When the Amazon Dash button was introduced in 2015, it was initially promoted as a consumer friendly way to reorder common household products. The Bluetooth-enabled ordering button would stick to any surface and offer an easy way to reorder products like paper towels or laundry detergent at the touch of a button. It sold at first.

Across the second half of 2015, Amazon sold over 400,000 Dash buttons, of which more than 25 percent were for three P&G brands – Tide, Bounty and Gillette. Despite the initial interest, though, market research firm Slice Intelligence estimated that less than half of people who purchased the button actually used it to complete an order, and those who did use it only made a purchase roughly once every two months.

So when Amazon nearly tripled the number of brand products available with Dash buttons and expanded the program in late 2016, some analysts were confused. Why expand a program that was seeing such limited results?

Amazon spokeswoman Kinley Pearsall acknowledged in an interview with the *Wall Street Journal* shortly after the announcement that the idea of people having houses full of buttons for each product was silly, but shared that the real vision was "that you never have to worry about hitting that button."

This is what automated consumerism could look like – a world where technology anticipates what you need, reorders it and has it delivered to your home without you even thinking about it (see Chapter 15 on the *Self Aware Data* trend). Baked into this idea is a sort of forced brand loyalty where consumers end up locked into a brand simply because it happens to be the one that was available or most visible at the time when they first placed an order.

Loyalty by extension would become something that a consumer is assigned rather than something they willfully choose. It would be passive instead of active.

Of course, considering loyalty as passive is much easier when you think about a commodity like laundry detergent or paper towels. What about when it comes to something more integral to our lives? What about if we consider our career and the workplace?

## The Myth Of Employee Satisfaction

In April of 2016 the results of the MetLife Annual U.S. Employee Benefit Trends Study were released with the optimistic finding that for the first time in years, employee loyalty was on the rise. The "rise" celebrated by the study was from 41% to 45%. In other words, when asked whether they planned to stay at their jobs beyond the next 12 months, *only* 45% answered yes.

That sort of statistic, when framed the opposite way, is hardly worthy of celebration. When less than half of your employees want to be there a year from now, is that really the sort of news that should inspire confidence? Sadly, when the bar for employee loyalty is so low, the honest answer is often yes.

One study from Bain & Company, for example, found that the average company could lose anywhere from 20% to 50% of its employee base each year. Yet for every statistic indicating that employees are likely to leave and unhappy in their roles, there is another such as the recent finding from the Society of Human Resource Management (SHRM) that concluded 88% of U.S. employees report overall job satisfaction.

At first, this probably seems like a strange contradiction. If people are satisfied, why do they seem to be jumping from job to job so quickly? Satisfaction is not the same thing as loyalty.

All these "satisfied" employees are actually just exhibiting *Passive Loyalty*. They are loyal until something better shows up, and then they leave. They don't hate their jobs or their companies, but they don't love them either. And if the opportunity for career advancement, or higher pay, or better benefits comes along … they will jump ship and leave.

## Why It Matters

For years marketers and business leaders have treated loyalty as a binary idea – you were either loyal, or you weren't. Today we are starting to understand that there is more nuance in the idea of loyalty, and passive loyalty is all around us – in our jobs, the things we buy and how we engage or don't engage with brands.

The real problem is that the customer loyalty *industry* – where brands are encouraged to fund and launch complex loyalty programs and dream up new opportunities to reward customers – is not necessarily adept at creating or encouraging *active* brand loyalty. Satisfied customers are not the same as loyal customers. Good performing satisfied employees are not necessarily loyal employees.

Rather than seeing this as a negative, though, the smart leaders and organizations are understanding that *passive* loyalty is just another stage of the journey towards *active* loyalty. Passively loyal customers are better than disloyal customers, or haters, or the indifferent who have no idea you exist. The business opportunity is to operationalize ways to transform these people – whether they are consumers or employees – into being actively loyal instead.

## How To Use This Trend:

✓ **Segment into passively and actively loyal**. If you can't tell your truly loyal customers or employees from the ones who would leave the first time they get a better offer – this is the first place you need to focus. Of course, making this distinction isn't easy, and it doesn't always match up nicely with tenure or spend. There are behaviors, indicators and analytics to understand or even predict the migration down to passive or up to active loyalty. Instead, you need to build your own "ultimate questions" to help you measure this. One example might be asking, "if we could keep your business for the next two years, what would we need to do?" These sorts of questions can help you get a deeper sense of who's actually loyal and who is going to leave they next chance they get.

✓ **Earn loyalty not sales** – If you preorder a book on Amazon. com and the price drops, they will send you a refund – even if it happens to be 17 cents. This consistency of unsolicited follow up builds intense trust among customers. There are many people who would never preorder a book from anyone else. And each time Amazon proactively sends back a few cents when a price drops, they continue to earn this loyalty. That's the difference between doing something worthy of loyalty and simply focusing on selling a product once.

✓ **Activate into active loyalty** – Once you know who your active vs passively loyal customers are, the good news is there are plenty of ways you could convert them. Getting actively loyal might come from finding ways to increase the switching cost so it doesn't seem so low or easy. Another is to encourage passively loyal customers to cash in on rewards or other things they have earned as a way to provide concrete evidence of what they are getting from you in a way that is more memorable. Finally, using more analytics and crafting the right strategy to get more insights from the data can also help you to convert customers into actively loyal customers.

# Chapter 8

# AUTHENTIC FAMESEEKERS

## *What's the Non-Obvious Trend?*

**A new generation of creators become authentic fameseekers – turning to social media to establish their brands, earn eyeballs and become the next big thing.**

For more than a decade, Oprah Winfrey was one of the most influential media personalities in the world. Her daily talk show had legions of loyal viewers, and her empire was on the rise. Brands would pay to try and win her attention, because her endorsement was golden. Consumers trusted her advice so implicitly that whenever she recommended a product or service, millions of people would flock to it.

This happened with such predictable frequency that the marketing world even coined a term for it: the "Oprah Effect."

The Oprah Effect sold millions of books, cosmetics, consumer products and food. It launched the careers of entrepreneurs, authors and innovators. Oprah Winfrey was the perfect example of what marketing people call an "influencer" – someone who can get people to act based on their recommendations.

Today the definition of an influencer has changed.

Now the most common description of an influencer is anyone who seems to have any sort of audience – whether that audience is an engaged, devoted fan or an idle YouTube subscriber who clicked a button once three years ago and forgot about it.

This new definition of influencers includes a huge new category of *Authentic Fameseekers*, people who have achieved their influence by finding innovative ways to attract eyeballs on social media, often through creating highly personal and authentic content.

Sometimes they have real talent. Other times the question of whether or not their skill should even be called talent is the subject of debate – like the creator of the most popular YouTube channel on Earth.

## The Curious Popularity Of PewDiePie

When 26 year old Swedish gamer Felix Kjellberg, created his first YouTube account in 2010 – he decided to name it after a combination of the sound that lasers in video games make (pew) and what you do after they fire (die). Then he forgot his password and was locked out – so he created another account adding one more three letter word to the end: "pie."

This laughably silly backstory is the perfect introduction to the mind of the controversial creator of the popular YouTube channel "PewDiePie" – the number one most popular channel on YouTube with over 47 million subscribers (more than twice the population of Australia).

His videos are usually a combination of profanity tinged gameplay videos and politically incorrect jokes. His style has been described simultaneously by *Variety* editor Andrew Wallenstein as "aggressive stupidity," and Yahoo! reporter Rob Walker as "raucous and crude." Yet his appeal, according to Walker, might come from the fact that he "always comes across as genuine. He addresses his audience as a bunch of peer-like friends."

Living up to this characterization, in a profile article from 2015 after news came out that Kjellberg makes approximately $7.4 million, the YouTuber released a personable and honest video about how he sees money, why he's not embarrassed and a simple explanation for his puzzling rise to stardom: "many people see me as a friend they can chill with for 15 minutes a day. The loneliness in front of the computer screens brings us together. But I never set out to be a role model; I just want to invite them to come over to my place."

Analyzing his success, journalist Ross Miller wrote, "love it or hate it, his success — like so many other YouTube personalities — isn't just in playing games but actually connecting and talking directly to an audience. No agent, press release, or any other intermediary. He just hit record."

This is the *Authentic Fameseeker* model of influence – where anyone can seek and achieve fame based primarily on his or her willingness to be authentic, flawed and human publicly in a way that respects and engages their audience.

For all his faults, PewDiePie clearly has a keen sense of how to build his own community of fans – whom he refers to as the "Bro Army." His example is inspiring other creators to seek the same kind of fame for themselves – often on YouTube as well.

## YouTube Entrepreneurs + Sponsors

In mid-2016, Google estimated that over 300 hours of video are uploaded to YouTube every minute and there are nearly 5 billion videos viewed on the platform worldwide every day.

70% of the site's users come from outside the U.S. and there are 10,113 videos that have generated over 1 billion views each. Those videos have paid out more than $1 billion to rights holders since 2007.

The site is a well known discovery platform for talented young musicians and some of the biggest music stars of the past decade including Justin Beiber, Katy Perry, Ed Sheeran, 5 Seconds of Summer and dozens of others were all first discovered on the site. Their stories have inspired a new generation of aspiring musicians to use the site to upload their own cover versions of popular songs and create their own channels in the hopes of being discovered themselves.

This hope goes well beyond musicians.

About six years ago around the same time Oprah said goodbye to her long running talk show, a small startup conference called VidCon quietly brought a few hundred of the most prolific video content creators on the Internet together. Wallenstein, the same *Variety* editor who panned PewDiePie, described that inaugural gathering of aspiring and current YouTube stars as "the next Comic-Con."

In the six years since, the event has delivered on that prediction. The 7th annual edition this past June in Anaheim, California attracted over 400 creators and more than 30,000 attendees. The sessions at the event focused on topics such as "When Everyone Matters – The New Ecology of Fandom," "How To Ask For Money From Your Audience," and "How To Brand Your Channel."

One of the biggest underlying beliefs of the event was the idea that anyone could be a creator, find their own fans, build a brand and make money on YouTube. This belief is so widespread that thousands of aspiring creators are trying to create channels for themselves and taking advantage of new learning opportunities to make connection in the industry with established video bloggers.

Over the past summer, there were several high profile camp experiences like "Creator Camp" in Wisconsin and 2bcamp for Spanish language speakers in Madrid which were hosted by popular video bloggers and designed to teach kids how to launch their own YouTube channels, build an audience and become a celebrity online themselves.

This quest for celebrity has extended to some of the hottest new social media platforms beyond YouTube as well.

All of these influencers flocking to YouTube has not gone unnoticed by brands either. For the past two years, P&G brand Tide detergent has partnered with popular YouTube stars to create a series of videos where all sorts of clothes are soiled in interesting ways. Then the stars use Tide and the clothing comes out perfectly clean.

Other brands like Coca-Cola, Samsung, L'Oreal and many others are all creating similar efforts to sponsor rising YouTubers. There are even platforms like Grapevine.com that help influencers get brand sponsorships by creating a marketplace where brands can "connect with the world's best creators."

# Beyond YouTube

When former movie producer Amanda Micallef started her online network called ArsenicTV – the vision she landed on with co-Founder and former Creative Artists Agency agent Billy Hawkins was entirely based on Snapchat. The "network" would feature a rotating series of models who would control ArsenicTV's account entirely during their shoots – editing and posting their own photos directly onto the account.

Micallef's reasoning was simple: "There's a nuance when you look at a picture of a girl when she's feeling empowered and beautiful — her hair is the way she wants, she's wearing what she wants, she's standing the way she wants — that's very different than when a guy is like 'stand there, turn your cheek that way,' and projecting what he thinks is sexy."

The idea was risqué, unusual and highly successful. The site receives more than a thousand submissions each day from aspiring models and all of them agree to post their photos entirely for free simply for the chance to garner tens of thousands of new followers to their own social media platforms from the exposure. Meanwhile the channel has more than half a million people clicking every photo and video and has already turned down a buyout offer from Playboy Enterprises.

ArsenicTV is just one emerging example of a platform that is attracting a new kind of influencer and creator – but there are plenty of others for everything from infomercials to video gaming:

- Twitch is one of the biggest online networks where gamers stream themselves playing video games for an eager and often adoring audience. The site was acquired by Google.YouTube in 2014 and averages 60,000 to 70,000 concurrent viewers on each live cast.
- Smosh Games is another platform for gamers and has the fourth most subscribed-to YouTube channel in the world with close to 7 million subscribers and more than 2 billion video views.
- Mik Mak is a mobile video shopping network available on Instagram where comedians and other entertainers record 30

second infomercials for brands to sell all kinds of products from eye cream to hot sauce.

- Wattpad is a platform that encourages fans of celebrities and series to create fan fiction and the site has more than 250 million original story uploads from over 2 million creators.
- Operator.com is a community of advisors who help you discover and buy products and offers access to experts in categories from fashion to electronics and personal shopping advice.
- Facebook has invested heavily in its Live platform designed to let anyone (including influencers) share real time video.

Each of these sites offers an opportunity for the *Authentic Fameseekers*, to build a personal brand and use it to earn their own sponsorships or advertising revenues. Sometimes these new breed of fameseekers are overt in their desire to court brands. In other cases, the brands pursue them – simply following the eyeballs and attention they have earned from consumers.

## Why It Matters:

It is a frequently heard criticism of Kim Kardashian (and by extension her entire family) that they are famous simply for being famous. After all, what *talent* do any of them really possess? But dismissing Kim Kardashian or her sisters merely as opportunists getting rich based on their good looks and willingness to pose for photos in various stages of undress misses an important point.

The underappreciated "talent" of the Kardashians is their ability to share the most intimate details of their own lives in a way that is mesmerizingly and authentically human. Even when you want to look away, you can't help but sneak a glance in their direction. They are *Authentic Fameseekers*, and their example has shaped the ideal of fame for a new generation of creators ready to post videos on Instagram, live stream game play and create the next great YouTube channel with extreme authenticity themselves.

The ultimate skill, it seems, is a willingness to offer an extreme version of personality and authenticity directly to fans … and then having the right business model and strategy to leverage this trend.

## How To Use This Trend:

✓ **Embrace emerging influencers** - When companies think about influencers, it is easy to look for and be too directly guided by numbers. There are more influencers creating platforms every day, but their numbers are not always "viral." Instead of chasing views or impressions, consider the emerging influencer who has built a small but loyal audience and engage them before they get big.

✓ **Think outside the platform** - One fascinating thing you will notice about the people creating their own audiences is that they tend to think in multi-channels. An Instagram star is also on Snapchat. YouTube stars will also use Twitter. The point is – there is a value in thinking about multiple platforms as a unified opportunity rather than setting up ideas to execute within each platform individually.

✓ **Do an authenticity audit** – What makes the Authentic Fameseeker so influential is the combination of creating something interesting and the underlying devotion to authenticity. This authenticity is something that companies need to uncover and use as well. It may seem difficult, but when I first wrote about this topic back in 2008 with my first book Personality Not Included, a critical first step came down to using the right process to create an "audit" of personality and authenticity.  This approach lets you pinpoint exactly where you might be losing trust and how to build it back by changing how you communicate and also which influencers you choose to work with.

# Chapter 9

# LOVABLE UNPERFECTION

## (ORIGINALLY CURATED 2014)

———

## *What's the Non-Obvious Trend?*

**As people seek out more personal and human experiences, brands and creators intentionally focus on using personality, quirkiness and intentional imperfections to make their products and experiences more human, authentic and desirable.**

When the Swedish Tourist Association wanted to celebrate the 250th anniversary of the country's abolishment of censorship last year, the group landed on a unique idea. To illustrate the government's dedication to transparency, they created a phone number for the country – and invited regular Swedes to volunteer to answer phone calls.

The entire campaign was simply known as "The Swedish Number" and on April 6th, 2016 the phone line went live with an open invitation for anyone around the world to call. Predictably, some of the first people to call were curious journalists looking to see if it was real and exactly how it worked so they could write about it. The resulting stories said much about the idea, execution and vision behind the campaign ... and about the country itself.

One reporter called and coincidentally ended up speaking with another reporter *from* Sweden who was on the other end also trying out the service with the intent of writing about it. Another writer spoke with a student in Sweden who was originally from Uganda and offered an outsider's view of the country.

In each case – the country's experiment in radical transparency proved the point that Sweden was a place for authentic uncensored self-expression. Both de facto Ambassadors admitted to having had no training, no instructions and no rules to follow. They just signed up online, picked a time and they were part of the program.

The fact that it happened to be Sweden trying this unique experiment should not have been that surprising.

The country had already made waves four years earlier with its bold attempt at transparency on Twitter by turning over control of the country's @sweden Twitter account to a new Swedish citizen every day. That initiative, called "Curators of Sweden" had its share of issues, but still continues today – featuring a new Swede every week.

What the Swedish Tourist Association knows is a lesson that many other brands, governments, associations and people are discovering ... that there is a beauty in having flaws and being willing to share them.

This is the essence of the *Lovable Unperfection* trend – where a form of radical transparency allows people and organizations to share their truthful story along with flaws and earn trust specifically for that reason.

## A Short History Of Unperfection

Avid readers of my previous trend reports may notice that this is a trend that I featured in various ways for two consecutive years – the only such trend in my seven years of predictions.

In 2014 I called this trend *Lovable Imperfection*. In 2015 I named a similar trend *Unperfection*. The difference between them at that point was that the first year was mainly focused on connecting with people while the second year applied more to businesses trying to be "strategically unperfect" through making their products or services purposefully flawed.

When it focused on people – the examples I used were well known villain characters from popular films or television like Walter White in Breaking Bad or Gru in Despicable Me.

In the year after – my description of the trend evolved to also describe brands creating manufactured products like Oscar Meyer sandwich meats, or imperfect brands like Ugg Boots or Crocs which have ardent fans despite the look of their footwear.

This year, I have put the two together to make *Lovable Unperfection*. But why include a trend that has already been covered in two previous trend reports once again – and what's different? The truth is, I hesitated to include it again … but the more I talked about the trend at conferences and had roundtable discussions with executives on the topic – the more convinced I became to include it once more.

It's not the same as it was, though. The most powerful companies and leaders today use the right process to exhibit a radical form of authenticity that endears them to their audiences. This usually involves sharing vulnerability and being willing to fail publicly in order to build trust. Let's take a look at a few examples of this in action.

## Behind The Scenes Video

When Fast Food chain Wendy's wanted to show customers where the ingredients in its salad come from, the brand put a GoPro camera on a head of lettuce and tracked its progress from the farm to the restaurant. The resulting video was posted on YouTube and watched over 7 million times.

A few years earlier when McDonald's was asked on Twitter why the burgers in their ads rarely resembled the ones served to customers, Canadian marketing manager Hope Bagozzi created a YouTube video showing what a photo shoot for McDonald's is really like. The three and a half minute video has been viewed more than 11 million times so far.

Over the past year, brands from automotive manufacturers to global fashion labels are all creating their own versions of videos to take people behind the scenes for how they make the things we buy. Many of them use raw unedited footage to exhibit a truthful unfiltered side that only rarely comes out.

In entertainment, this is the same model that martial arts star Jackie Chan used for more than two decades to build his audience. At the end of each of his films, there are a series of outtake of him attempting and failing the stunts from his film. Those outtakes endear him, show his daring personality and make him more human.

And then there is the example of the most confusingly honest hotel in the world – which has been winning for over a decade by promoting the one thing no other hotel would.

## Hans Brinker Budget Hotel

Imagine for a moment if you are the marketing director in charge of a considerably seedy backpacker hotel in Amsterdam. The property you are responsible for promoting is so spartan that most frills people might expect at even a backpacker style accommodation are missing.

If you were like most travel marketers, you might decide to find a great photographer with a very wide angle lens and hope for the best. Then you might focus your marketing on some other angle, such as cost or location.

For Hans Brinker Budget Hotel in Amsterdam, the right strategy ended up being exactly the opposite: embrace their awfulness and talk about it honestly. For more than 15 years, the hotel has been promoting itself as the "worst hotel in the world."

The brand advertising features unapologies like "sorry for being excellent at losing your luggage," and "sorry for being the best in ignoring your complaints." Another ad promises that staying there will "improve your immune system," due to the hotel's ambient slovenliness. When the brand opened a second location in Lisbon, the taglines for the new property promised the "same lack of social skills, different accent."

As anyone who has ever worked on promoting a destination or travel property knows, sometimes expectations can set you up for failure. Frequent fliers expect to be upgraded to a seat they didn't pay for, and then get angry when they are not. Patrons of luxury hotels expect perfection, and often feel justified to complain about any little thing, no matter how small. The unusual solution, reasoned Hans Brinker's agency KesselsKramer when first proposing the campaign, was to lower expectations to a point where people could no longer be disappointed. Thus the concept of the "worst hotel in the world" was born.

The hotel uses innovative posters and direct marketing to promote their "experience" to their target audience of young backpackers. After all, what twenty-something wouldn't want to return home to boast to their friends and family that they stayed in the worst hotel in the world while in Amsterdam?

The campaign has turned the property's biggest negative attribute into the only reason for people to stay. And it has worked, as the hotel is routinely full and raved about on social media (for their marketing, not so much for the experience). Their success has even led to a coffee table book featuring over a decade of their entertaining advertising.

What's the lesson in this? Sometimes an extreme form of honesty and a healthy dose of *Lovable Unperfection* can be the ultimate competitive advantage.

## Why It Matters:

We no longer live in a world where everyone feels the necessity to always strive for perfection. In examples from behind the scenes videos to boldly talking about a pitiful hotel experience, this idea of making purposefully flawed products, services and experiences as a way to make them unique and desirable is gaining popularity. What it means for all of us is that the emotional and personal aspects of an experience that make it memorable may be the exact same ones that might previously have been considered imperfect. The challenge for any of us will be to let unperfection moments exist and delight customers with them instead of desperately trying to remove them.

# How To Use This Trend:

✓ **Embrace your "flaws"** – For listeners of National Public Radio, Diane Rehm has one of the most easily recognizable voices on air. Her voice is the byproduct of her long struggle with a neurological condition known as spasmodic dysphonia, which affects the tone of her voice. Yet Rehm's flawed voice is part of her personality and charm, and it helps her stand out. Amongst a sea of perfect altos reading the news, her voice offers something different, and millions of loyal listeners reward her for it with their attention.

✓ **Flawed is different than broken** – It may be tempting to see this trend as permission to do things badly. That would be a mistake. The power of *Lovable Unperfection* does not come from refusing to fix broken things or offering a substandard experience or product. Even the Hans Brinker actually offers working plumbing and a real bed to sleep in, despite what their ads say. If you have something that's broken, you need to fix it. But being strategically flawed – that can help you stand out in an unexpected way.

✓ **Make flaws a selling point** - Since 2015 Walmart has had a program to sell "ugly" fruits and vegetables in a bid to reduce food wastage – including weather-damaged apples and "Spuglies" (misshapen and smaller potatoes). Furniture salesmen have long described distinctive wood textures as unique and valuable rather than flawed. This same tactic might work for your brand as well.

# Chapter 10

# PRESERVED PAST

## *What's the Non-Obvious Trend?*

**Technology offers new ways for us to preserve history, changing the way that we learn from, experience and shape the past.**

What if we had the ability to capture any real world experience and preserve it forever?

The desire to save and remember the present has been around for most of recorded human history. In the past 100 years we have gotten far more visual with this desire, thanks to photography and video, but none of these have come close to offering a really immersive historical experience.

For a deeper immersion, you could always visit ancient ruins or participate in a historical reenactment – but these still only offer a limited view. When it comes to recording our own lives, we can come a bit closer to reliving history because we evoke our own memories of actually being there through selfies and videos captured mostly on our phones.

But what about the places around us and the history that they hold which is usually hidden from view? If you consider the ambition of Toronto based virtual reality innovator The Third Fate – we would find more opportunities to immerse ourselves in the past if we got better at capturing and saving the present.

The award winning design studio has used its 360 degree capture technology recently to preserve once-in-a-lifetime experiences like artist Bjarke Ingel's BIG Maze at the National Building Museum in Washington DC as well as everyday cityscapes like Manhattan's Columbus Circle. The studio's vision is to use technology to preserve structures slated for demolition or renovation, buildings in decay, changing landscapes, new builds and exhibitions.

If you think about it, this desire to use technology to record the present so we might experience and enjoy it far into the future isn't that different than the reason any of us record our lives through selfies and videos. There is a beautiful power in the *Preserved Past*, and this trend is about much more than just recording an experience. Technology may be able to help us make sure we don't leave the past behind as well.

Drones, virtual and augmented reality, 3D imagery, and cutting edge design are all being applied to preserve the past in various ways. The beautiful side effect is that these initiatives are also making the past easier to experience and access on demand, often alongside the present.

This is the *Preserved Past* – a world where we can access, experience and learn from our shared past more easily and with a new level of immersiveness, insight and connection.

## Living History

The easiest place to start an exploration of this trend is with museums because they are already destinations that curate the past. Around the world, forward looking museums are evolving to rapidly becoming more than dusty buildings where artifacts are stored behind glass cases. At the Acropolis Museum in Greece, for example, one team is using technology to bring a collection of architectural and sculptural remains to life with augmented reality (AR) to restore colors and lost features.

At The Dali Museum in Florida, an exhibit called "Dreams of Dali" allows visitors to use a virtual reality headset to step inside and explore the artist's 1935 painting *Archeological Reminiscence of Millet's Angelus.* Every detail of the painting has been lovingly recreated for anyone to experience as if they were entering the strange abstract world of Dali's mind in real time.

Of course, recreating historical artifacts or taking a tour inside an artist's mind are not the same as speaking with someone directly. The problem usually is that this type of conversation is impossible to have – but one project is even creating a solution for that constraint with an unusual idea.

The effort is called New Dimensions In Testimony (NDT) and was developed as a collaboration between several groups at the University of Southern California (USC) to add a human face to one of the darkest times in human history.

The demo project features real Holocaust survivor Pinchas Gutter being asked to answer nearly 2,000 questions about his experience and life. While being interviewed, the project used 50 cameras arranged in a rig to capture a three-dimensional recording of him telling his story across an entire week.

These responses were then indexed using natural language processing software and a hologram was created with his likeness for people to interact with. The result is a fascinating and slightly unnerving experience of actually having a conversation with a Holocaust survivor ... something we can still do today, but that will be impossible a mere 10 or 15 years from now.

What all this innovation illustrates is that the history which we once learned from books and the occasional school field trip to look at paintings on museum walls is becoming interactive, deeper and vastly more personal than ever before.

## Augmented Reality Travel

Experiencing the past is also becoming more widely available to people outside the confines of museum exhibits.

One of the earliest examples of this was an app called StreetMuseum from The Museum of London first launched more than six years ago. The app allows users to walk through the streets of London and use their mobile device to overlay paintings and arts of work over the actual scene and location they are passing through in order to see what the city once looked like.

Similar Augmented Reality Tours include everything from the "Paris, Then and Now" app, to the "PIVOTtheWorld" app which offers a mobile tour of the Harvard campus with historical markers to tell the story of what the school was like centuries ago.

Augmented reality is also being rapidly adopted by brands in the Travel and Tourism sector. Best Western Hotels & Resorts launched a virtual experience where consumers can see into rooms, amenities and locations. Last year Asian hotel brand Shangri-La announced it would be doing something similar targeted at travel agents and meeting planners.

Hilton, Marriott, and Starwood (the latter two brands having recently merged) have all launched their own pilot programs with augmented reality. On the airline side, United and Lufthansa are both using VR to show off their interior cabins – while Qantas is making inflight VR entertainment available.

All these nascent efforts from so many brands inspired consulting firm Deloitte to dub 2016 the "year of experimentation" in its expansive report on the state of the virtual reality industry. But you might be wondering what does all this experimentation have to do with the *Preserved Past*?

The fascinating side effect of all this focus on cataloging experiences as they are today is just how much visual history is being created for tomorrow. All the experimentation is giving us a visual record of what hotels, public spaces, and even airplane seats look like today—and this will be interesting visual content for the future. That is, assuming someone at all these brands decides it is worth saving and preserving for the future.

## The History Of Brands

It might seem like wishful thinking to expect notoriously short sighted companies to volunteer to maintain their own archives for historical value. When it comes to history, though, a growing number of brands are taking a page from museums and already launching their own storytelling initiatives focused on retelling and preserving the past.

When 600 year old soy sauce brand Kikkoman commissioned a short documentary from director Lucy Walker to tell the story of its long history, many skeptics questioned the move. The film was called "Make Haste Slowly" and lasted a luxurious 24 minutes. The length (and topic) caused critics to wonder about its utility. After all, who would really sit down and watch a long film about the history of soy sauce?

When asked about the film, Morgan Spurlock (director of the product placement exposé film *The Greatest Movie Ever Sold*) agreed most people wouldn't rush out to see a film on soy sauce, but also noted that "if you're using this as a historical document, there could be some great storytelling to come out of it."

The underlying desire to combine corporate history with great storytelling has become the ambition for other forward looking brands as well.

The motorcycle brand Harley Davidson recently launched a three part miniseries on *The Discovery Channel*. Delta Airlines is working with StoryCorps to interview customers and capture employee's stories. Cognac maker Rémy Martin uses an interactive website to allow anyone to experience 300 years of brand history in a matter of minutes.

As more marketing teams around the globe shift their attention from promotions and advertising to storytelling and content – the brands with powerful historical stories are finding new ways to leverage their backstories and use them to engage consumers.

When longtime Coca-Cola executive Rebecca Messina left to take on the Chief Marketing Officer role at Beam Suntory – she noted "it was through our archives at Coke that I was able to create some of the best stories we created at Coke. What drew me [to the Beam Suntory job] were brands with insane histories. In a world where stories and authenticity are more important than ever, you can't walk into a business better positioned for that world."

Her vision which she shared in an interview with *Forbes* shortly after taking on her role is to take some of those iconic Beam Suntory brands – like Jim Beam, Maker's Mark, Courvoisier, Yamazaki, Hakushu and Hibiki – and bring their histories to life.

The more brands I work with to add more storytelling to their marketing – the more I see them embracing their past. We are already seeing more museum-worthy campaigns and stories worth preserving far into the future as an important and fascinating homage to the good and bad role consumerism and brands have played throughout human history.

## Careers Of The Future

One of the most fascinating elements of the *Preserved Past* trend is how it is inspiring new career paths and innovative fields of study. Take the emerging field of "Forensic Architecture," for example, which involves combining everything from mobile-phone footage from regular people to the size of smoke plumes to recreate the scenes of human rights controversies or wartime actions.

The worldwide leader in the space, known simply as Forensic Architecture (FA), is led by 45-year-old Israeli professor Eyal Weizman out of Goldsmiths, University of London. He describes his chosen field as "not cold science. This is committed, engaged, citizen science … people's memory records, the grass records, the trees record, the plumes in the air record, the concrete records. Everything is recording in a variable way."

So FA has pioneered ways of measuring these once dispersed records and merging them to understand what really happened in war zones, refugee crisis or natural disasters. The resulting reports are frequently used by prosecutors working on cases of human rights violations. They also create a rare portrait of the past that filters out the commonplace historical bias that comes when victors write the history of nations while looking backward after celebrating conquest.

Another industry of the feature is "Digital Conservation" where teams across the world are moving quickly to catalog and save endangered archaeology from being destroyed by mass tourism and the rise of militant extremist groups.

Factum Arte is a team of "digital conservators" who are using a combination of 3D scanners and teams of young tech-savvy girls to take photos of historical landmarks before they disappear forever. In the words of Factum Arte director Adam Lowe, "the goal is 1000 people taking 1000 photos every day. The idea is you record vast amounts of cultural heritage. You have to be proactive and lay the grounds to record the data that's at risk, and do it fast."

Others like ScanLAB, a London-based studio, are using 3D technology to map underground worlds that would otherwise be inaccessible and make them accessible in digital ways. And several University based teams are exploring the practice of "Drone Mapping" as a way to create topographical maps of places that are either unreachable or extremely dangerous for humans to go. These maps are used for everything from helping guide archaeologists around shipwrecks to planning evacuation routes at large concert venues.

"Forensic architecture," "digital conservation," "endangered archaeology" and "drone mapping" are just a few of the up and coming industries that all deal in some way with creating a new model for preserving our understanding of our past. All of them are a symbol of the impact that this trend is starting to have not only on how we understand the past, but also in how many people might eventually make that journey a central part of their careers.

## Why It Matters:

As a part of my work as a trend curator, I am lucky to be invited to many events where I see and engage with innovators doing things that are likely to change the industries in which they work. For the past 5 years, one of my favorite events consistently has been the Future of Storytelling held in the unique location of Snug Harbor Cultural Center on Staten Island in New York. The event gathers a menagerie of business people, creative artists, brands, technologists and other futurists engaging for four days in exploring the evolution of storytelling for businesses, change agents and creative artists. At the latest gathering, a key theme on display was how many of the technologies and initiatives driving the *Preserved Past* trend are fundamentally shifting how organizations tell their stories and engage consumers with immersive media -- augmented reality, virtual reality or mixed reality. The biggest takeaway from the event is that these tools, when used properly and not as a gimmick, can offer a powerful new media to express, inspire and move people into action.

Over the past year, we have steadily moved from a natural fascination with the past to a multi-faceted quest to understand and preserve it on multiple levels. As new technology such as 3D scanners and drone technology start merging with mainstay disciplines like archaeology or architecture – entirely new industries and opportunities are emerging. We also have more ways than ever to preserve the history of our own lives through social media. Along the way, all of us are benefitting from the exchange with more ways to experience and understand the past as we travel virtually or physically through the beauty of the world. The past is becoming new again, which means our understanding of it can finally become deeper and it can play a bigger role in our current lives as well.

## How To Use This Trend:

✓ **Preserve the present** – You may not have the ego to consider anything you do on an everyday basis worthy of saving for historical purposes – but we can all find ways to help support those who are choosing to spend time and effort preserving the present. Just be a consumer and evangelist for the information they save and the experiences they create.

✓ **Share the past** – Given the number of new tools available to appreciate the past, you can certainly make it a larger part of any travel experience and share that same experience with fellow family members or travelers. Using these tools can transform a place into a magical experience when traveling.

✓ **Feature your people** – Beyond telling stories of products or company history, employee stories can also offer a wealth of content to increase engagement with consumers and also making recruiting great people even easier. The stories can also help to share the evolution of an organization and be useful for PR efforts, archives, cultural lore, marketing and training purposes.

# Chapter 11

# DEEP DIVING

---

## *What's the Non-Obvious Trend?*

While our shrinking attention span leads people to consume information more selectively, many people prefer to dive deeply into
experiences that truly capture their interest.

"Humans have a shorter attention span than goldfish!"

This was the breathless headline across global media a few years ago
when a team of Canadian researchers surveyed two thousand people and
found the average human attention span had dropped from about 12 seconds in the year 2000 (when mobile phone adoption was just starting to
take off) to 8 seconds in 2016. In comparison, goldfish are believed to
have an attention span of nine seconds ... so reporters had their perfect
linkbaiting headline.

In response to this new reality, everyone from the media to advertisers struggled to create "snackable" content (as it was increasingly
called) for this new reality. My trend report from 2014 explored this
through a trend I called *Glanceable Content* – which described the

growing challenge for creators and brands to make their content immediately meaningful at a glance.

This imperative to make content glanceable was illustrated perfectly through the rise of the text-message inspired acronym, TLDR (Too Long, Didn't Read). Over the past few years, though, a curious counter trend has started to emerge. Not everything is too long to read. Some of it is too long to read *now*, but perfect to read *later*.

The idea of TLDR is slowly being replaced (or perhaps augmented) by the nuanced idea of TIRL (Too Interesting, Read Later). In other words, we are all becoming experts at parceling out our time to spend *more* of it selectively with the content that engages us the most deeply in the moments when we choose to make the time for it.

This is the shift at the heart of the *Deep Diving* trend – which explores why people choose to spend more time with some content, how they do it, and why it matters.

## Why People Love "Long Reads"

In the middle of 2016, the Pew Research Center released the results of a study to answer the burning question many in media and journalism has been asking for years: is the market for long form content dead?

Most of the media industry has resigned itself to the fact that impressions are still the gold standard for how advertisers buy space, which means unless people get smarter or manage to find new ways to resist clickbaiting headlines, Buzzfeed-style lists and devious 25 page slideshows to find out what childhood celebrities look like today will still be around.

Hardly a desirable future for media.

Thankfully, the conclusions of the study were startlingly optimistic. "When it comes to the relative time consumers spend with this content," the study concluded, "long-form journalism does have a place in today's mobile-centric society."

After months of reviewing 117 million anonymized cell phone interactions with 74,840 articles from 30 news websites in the month of September 2015 – the researchers learned that readers *do* spend about twice the time with long-form news content on their cellphones as with short-form. Alone that is not surprising considering long form content is, well, longer ... so of course it should take longer to read.

The interesting part came later in the study when they found that "return visitors to long-form articles spent 277 seconds with the article compared with 123 seconds for users overall." This one finding was key because it also illustrated a behavior that nearly every other study about our attention spans and media length tends to ignore – our penchant to save interesting things and return to them later.

Earlier in this article I called this "TIRL" to describe this idea that timing matters more than we often realize for how long people tend to spend diving more deeply into a piece of media or even engagement in advertising.

One of the smartest early media properties to cater specifically to this behavior was WIRED magazine when they created a section on their website for "long reads" (www.wired.com/tag/longreads). Rather than focus on up to the minute tech news, this section includes a collection of the magazine's most engaging long articles (regardless of publication date) – from an April 2016 article about Elon Musk's bold plans for artificial intelligence to a piece about the inspired teaching methods of a Mexican teacher named Sergio Juárez Correa first published in October 2013.

The stories there, despite being originally written for a monthly magazine, have become timeless – and perfect for readers who choose to spend longer pockets of free time engaging with an in depth piece of journalism. *The New York Times*, in response to this growing trend, also recently launched *Insider* – a news property sold as a "digital add on subscription that takes you behind the headlines for an unprecedented look inside The New York Times."

This trend of *Deep Diving* is extending beyond reading to what we watch on screen as well.

## Best. Show. Ever. Watch The Recap ...

For die-hard fans of the 1990s political drama *West Wing*, this past year's US election cycle has provided a combination of nostalgia and dread. Nostalgia for a show that portrayed exactly the sort of human, wise and kind President most people dream of having … and dread because it is fairly clear that an optimistic fictional character like that bears little resemblance to the politicians we will actually get into office.

For years, fans of the show have had to satisfy their nostalgia by watching reruns via internet streaming platforms like Netflix. This past year, though, former cast member Joshua Molina launched a podcast called *The West Wing Weekly* which promised to break down every episode of the hit drama as well as offer new interviews with former cast members and exclusive chats with all sorts of other personalities – including fans of the show. The podcast is offering exactly the kind of *Deep Diving* that new and old fans of the show love to engage with.

A similar example comes from comedians and TV writers Casey Wilson and her longtime collaborator Danielle Schneider, who are huge fans of the reality series *Real Housewives*. On a whim they started recording a podcast together from Wilson's kitchen table about the reality series and its 10 spinoff series in cities around the US and called it *Bitch Sesh*: A *Real Housewives Breakdown*. The show has become a cult hit.

The popular HBO hit drama series *Game Of Thrones* also has a recap show called *After The Thrones* where the hosts spend an hour dissecting the notoriously complex plot lines of the show and digging into the significance of each character's actions, reviewing scenes, and having exactly the kind of meticulous nuanced conversation about show trivia that only a super fan could love.

What each of these examples illustrates is how small subsets of audiences have a thirst for deep content about the experiences they love – and have a willingness to spend what might seem like an insane amount of time and often money indulging this experience.

## Wanderlust For The "Post-Tourist"

Just over a year ago an article by Thomas Rogers in *New York* magazine declared Berlin the "Post-Tourist Capital Of Europe." At that time the term "post-tourist" was just starting to emerge to describe a growing category of travelers who sought more real experiences while traveling by skipping the usual tourist hotspots, choosing to stay in AirBnbs or local homes instead of hotels, combining work with travel and immersing themselves in local culture as much as possible.

Berlin was a perfect place to explore the growth of this new type of travel because it was exactly the kind of growing destination where the rapid evolution was on clear display. Though the city has only 3.5 million people, it recently became the third-most-visited city in Europe, after London and Paris.

The post-tourist is one who stays for longer, immerses herself in the culture of a place and engages in a new form of Deep Diving that creates entirely new behaviours when traveling – including a willingness to get lost.

The Kompl app can indulge that desire for wandering by focusing on letting travelers take unexpected journeys by getting lost on purpose. The app uses sources like Foursquare and Wikipedia to highlight nearby attractions, but only shows where a destination is in relation to a traveler ... without any maps or turn by turn directions. Travelers then must explore and find the destination on their own.

The powerful idea behind the app is that sometimes the shortest distance to a destination might not be the most desirable or fun. Being more spontaneous and wandering allows for more serendipity and more interesting discoveries.

This encouraged wanderlust among the post-tourist and is also a perfect example of how *Deep Diving* can impact our real life choices. In a world filled with quick burst experiences, the future of travel seems to be something more meaningful, far deeper, and involving much more willful wandering.

The impact of this goes further than just the travel industry as well. *Deep Diving* is affecting how far consumers go to understand the sourcing and creation of some types of products, or go behind the scenes of entertainment based experiences.

## Why It Matters:

While media properties and brands alike have complained about the lack of attention span making it more difficult than ever to earn attention – consumers of information and experiences in all formats are finding their own ways to identify and spend time with the things they find most interesting and useful. Today, leading edge companies are already understanding where and how to create content tailored for the reader looking for a longer, deeper and more engaging experience. The smartest organizations are leveraging their backstories as a way to engage customers (both B2B and B2C) to go deeper, wander more and have more authentic experiences. Finally, brands in all industries will also start to realize that there is another way to capture attention beyond creating snackable content or paying the most for advertising. The lesson is simple: create something of value, present it skillfully and the right people will selectively spend all kinds of time and money on it.

## How To Use This Trend:

✓ **Find your backstory** – In many cases, the most engaging content you have is the backstory of why you do what you do and how you do it. TV shows have podcasts and video recaps that take you behind the episode. Luxury brand Hermès launched a film this past year that takes consumers inside one of their silk mills in Lyon France to illustrate how their product is really made. No matter what your story, if you can tell it in an interesting way – there will be an audience interested enough to spend time with you.

✓ **Create your own "TIRL" system** – As a consumer of media, you are bound to find stories or interesting content that are too involved to engage with in the moment but perfect to save and engage with later. When I start teaching my class at Georgetown, this is one of the first things they learn how to do. Through a combination of smart digital notetaking and a good old fashioned notebook, they understand how to curate their own content for later consumption.

✓ **Inventory your media** – When it comes to existing content and materials that already exist, there may be plenty of past work that could lend itself to extracting or adding more Deep

Diving worthy content. This is a tactic commonly used by film studios that have archival footage and past materials that may be able to experience a second life through online distribution. The point is, great brands understand that sometimes the most powerful content might already have been created and simply need someone to rediscover it.

# Chapter 12

# PRECIOUS PRINT
## (ORIGINALLY CURATED 2013)

---

## *What's the Non-Obvious Trend?*

**Thanks to our digital-everything culture, the few objects and moments we choose to interact with in print or physically become more emotionally valuable and deeply personal.**

In the American version of the popular comedy series "The Office," the blundering but lovable regional manager Michael Scott of paper supply company Dunder Mifflin (played by Steve Carell) decides to create an ad for the utility of his product. The ineffectually hilarious tagline he eventually lands upon, "limitless paper for a paperless world" is at once ironic, silly and profound.

The fact that we are heading towards a paperless world seems inevitable.

Every business leader hears about the need for "digital transformation" and doing away with old modes of business. Banks encourage consumers to get statements delivered via email. Airline boarding passes no longer need to be printed. And many newspapers and magazines are reducing circulation – or discontinuing their print editions altogether.

Four years ago I first wrote about a countertrend to our growing digital world and called it *Precious Print* to describe the growing sense that in a digital world, those few things in our lives which we chose to keep in printed form were becoming increasingly intentional, rare, valuable and even precious.

At the time when I first shared this trend, the examples I shared as evidence were mainly based on top tier printing solutions, the few magazines that embraced their printed roots out of tradition, and small businesses standing out for how they offered paper based experiences.

In 2017, this trend has grown far bigger than family photos and beautiful business cards. *Precious Print* is now a macro idea and trend that describes the evolution of entire industries from the resurgence of neighborhood bookstores to the explosion of art collecting. At the heart of each of these unlikely movements is the underappreciated magic of print in all its forms.

## The Middle Collector

The hobby and profession of art collection has had an elitist reputation for decades. Just mention art collecting and most people might conjure up a Hollywood image of well-dressed people holding up paddles at an auction to spend insane amounts of money on questionably artistic artifacts. One economist's exposé of the world of art recently published on *Quartz* justifiably called high-end art "one of the most manipulated markets in the world."

Yet the market for art is changing, thanks to several innovative startups who are working to make art collecting far less pretentious and more approachable. For example, startup website Paddle8.com was founded in 2011 to offer well-heeled consumers an alternative to the stuffy experience of the high end auction. The online auction platform chose to focus on the "mid-range" collector – offering works of art averaging around $5000 each, and the site later merged with longtime rival Auctionata.com to create one of the world's largest online auction marketplaces for art, with combined sales in 2015 of over $150 million.

When it comes to the broader world of art collecting, the industry leading Hiscox's Online Art Trade Report recently predicted revenue may grow to $6.3 billion by 2019, a threefold increase from 2014.

The numbers point to an interesting conclusion about what role art collection plays in modern culture. While much has been written about the younger generation's preference to share rather than own – when it comes to art, even younger consumers are actively choosing to invest in printed pieces they value as a financial and emotional investment.

## The Cult Of Paper

Of course, not all artistic ideas are meant to be hung on walls. Some of them are created through the simple act of putting pen to paper in order to capture an idea … in a notebook.

Notebooks today offer the ultimate homage to the emotional power of paper and the written word. From evangelic online user communities to ongoing memes encouraging people to share their drawings – notebooks from legendary makers like Moleskine, Leuchtturm and others have become the ultimate badge of honor of any creative person today. It is a decidedly popular analog habit for entrepreneurs and artists alike to pull out a worn paper notebook with pride to capture their handwritten notes, journal their thoughts or draw sketches to express ideas.

It turns out there is some science to support the idea that using notebooks instead of digital tools may even boost the memorability of ideas. In 2013 a Norwegian study of 10th graders clearly demonstrated that teens who read on computer screens understood less than those who read on paper. The researchers concluded that this could partially be due to the fact that "the brain has an easier task when you can touch as well as see."

American University Linguistics Professor Naomi S. Baron has gone a step further, spending five years examining the pros and cons of reading on-screen versus in print. Her survey research with University students in the United States, Germany and Japan revealed that "if cost were the same, about 90 percent prefer hard copy for schoolwork. If a text is long, 92 percent would choose hard copy."

Perhaps the most wide ranging defense of paper for the past several years has predictably come from a group with the most at stake – paper manufacturer Domtar. The brand's PAPERbecause campaign is a long running public advocacy effort on behalf of paper, but it also reminds us all of our human connection to paper.

Beyond the sentimental bias, the website goes on to present data and research about everything from how it is easier to learn on paper to how paper is one of the most recycled products on the planet.

Of course, a component of the campaign is in defense of direct mail, so clearly not all aspects of paper could be fairly described as "precious" – but the point is that important ideas shared on paper have a resonance, memorability and preciousness that ideas on digital often don't.

Especially when it comes to books.

## Why Argentineans Love Bookstores

Argentina is a fascinating place for any book lover.

The country boasts more bookstores per person than any other country on earth (734 for a population of 2.8 million) and its capital city Buenos Aires has more bookstores than any other city in the world. This prevalence of literary culture reaches every generation, as Antonio Dalto, business manager of the Ateneo Grand Splendid bookshop, shared in a recent interview about the Argentinean passion for books and bookstores.

"Culture is very important to the people of Buenos Aires," Dalto shared. "Even young kids read books, we see them here every day. Books for teenagers are one of our biggest sellers." The idea of young "digital natives" preferring books perhaps seems like the most counterintuitive of all. Kids are the ones driving the digital revolution, right?

The latest sales data from the publishing industry would seem to disprove that assumption.

Near the end of 2015, the entire industry was celebrating new numbers from Nielsen Bookscan that pointed to a slight rise in print book sales for the year. The news was widely celebrated as a sign that ebook sales may have plateaued and that there were plenty of people who preferred books – including young people (evidenced by the fact that teen fiction was one of the best-selling categories).

While some skeptics pointed out that some of the gains were partially due to the explosion of adult coloring books (which don't have ebook versions for obvious reasons), the popularity of print books seems for the moment to be on the rise. And the industry is responding.

UK-based Waterstones bookstore stopped selling Kindles and ebooks outside the UK, gave the shelf space to books instead and saw a 5% spike in sales.

In the U.S., beloved children's book author Judy Blume opened her own independent bookstore in Key West, Florida. When asked about her unexpected venture, Blume said: "I just think people are so hungry for a real bookstore again ... it's not just us doing well. A lot of independent booksellers are."

## Precious Unboxing

One of the most common ways that most of us interact with print without noticing is through product packaging. Most product packaging, though, could rarely be described as anything close to precious. The closest it usually comes are the beautifully ornate designs and packaging used for items like perfume or bottles of high end alcohol.

Usually, when you received a product with packaging worth lusting over, it was a moment to be enjoyed in private. When it comes to many high end consumer products like video gaming consoles or smartphones, that is no longer the case.

A simple search on YouTube for just about any popular recently released product will generate a stream of videos from ordinary users filming and posting their "unboxing" videos. The unboxing video is exactly what it sounds like – a user getting a product and filming the act of taking it out of the packaging and starting to test it out. Several years ago, the prevalence of these unboxing videos exploded – to the point where CNN published a story called "The Bizzare, Lucrative World of 'Unboxing' Videos."

One example is Tech video unboxing blogger Lewis Helsenteger, the creator of the "Unbox Therapy" video blog on YouTube which has over 6 million subscribers and over 900 million views of his videos since 2010. Another example from a different category is the MommyandGracieShow, a video blog run by a mother daughter team who unbox toys and dolls – and have more than 700,000 subscribers. The viral popularity of their videos even landed them an invitation to the industry Chicago Toy and Game Fair tradeshow to create a live unboxing video from the stage.

Unboxing as a category now officially even has its own Wiki to catalog who is doing unboxing and the rise of unboxing as a category.

Some unboxing videos rack up millions of views within days of a product being released. The videos also have a big influence on whether consumers buy a product or not because they are far more engaging and truthful than a simple three sentence review posted on Amazon. They are intimate, personal and highly persuasive – often celebrating the inherent preciousness of the print packaging itself.

## Why It Matters:

While it may seem counterintuitive, the digital revolution is actually making print more precious in those moments when we encounter or experience it. Sometimes that may come from the beautiful packaging of a product that we buy. Other times, it may be from the experience of just visiting a bookstore or library to browse the collection. Or we may choose to buy art that creates some emotional connection for us to put on a wall and transport us to a different time or place. Or it could come, as it does for many entrepreneurs and creative people, through that moment when they find a powerful idea and choose to write it down in a notebook and save it for later digestion. Regardless of the form, there are plenty of situations where print is the preferred medium for passionate engagement.

## How To Use This Trend:

✓ **Make your experience collectible**. Part of the appeal of print comes from the human desire for collections. We love to gather pieces of a puzzle together and enjoy the sense of achievement when we complete something. It is the reason for that moment of pleasure when you get another stamp in your passport at immigration, or why we still buy products in sets. To harness this trend, consider what aspect of your customer experience you might be able to make collectible in print, so customers would come back again and again to collect them.

✓ **Recognize VIPs with paper**. Nothing makes people feel as good as recognition. For your best customers, giving them discounts or greeting them by name every time they come to your location are great ideas ... but consider what you might be able to offer them in print. It might be a membership card, or a custom greeting mailed to their home for the holidays.

✓ **Create a culture book** – Zappos founder Tony Hseih is famous for creating a company culture book that is so iconic business professionals from all kinds of other industries have used it as an inspiration to create an internal culture worth evangelizing. The less appreciated fact about this Culture Book is that it is, in fact, a printed book and artifact that all employees receive as a tangible demonstration of just how important the corporate culture is. Creating a printed publication could help do the same for your organization.

# Chapter 13

# INVISIBLE TECHNOLOGY

## *What's the Non-Obvious Trend?*

The more sophisticated technology gets, the more it is able to anticipate needs, protect us and provide utility while increasingly blending unnoticeably into our daily lives.

Scott Jenson describes himself as a "battle tested veteran of the software industry." He has worked at Apple, holds over 20 patents and currently leads a group at Google focused on the mission of making everyday physical objects capable of broadcasting information to the web. This project, known simply as "Physical Web" has a broad mission statement to allow people to "walk up and use anything."

The idea that any object or place can broadcast content is on many levels an inevitable consequence of the Internet of Things (IoT). The difference between the Physical Web and IoT is that the objects and locations use something called a Bluetooth Low Energy (BLE) beacon to broadcast content over Bluetooth – thus removing the need for Internet connectivity.

In the process of evangelizing how this technology works, Jenson delivers keynote speeches to events filled with User Interface designers and is fond of telling stories. One of his favorites looks backward in history at the evolution of the car steering wheel and how the very first designs for cars were inspired by boats. As he told one audience at an event in 2014, "the first cars that were invented had the engine in the back … and the first steering wheel wasn't a steering wheel, it was a tiller."

He uses the tiller to make an analogy about how we often approach innovation. We usually start by creating something based on what we already know rather than something that works best. It was only when the tiller concept was replaced with a steering wheel that the popularity of cars started to take off and they realized their full potential.

The "technology tiller" analogy illustrates the problem of trying to merge new ideas with old systems, but also how important interface design has always been to the adoption curve for innovation. As technology gets more sophisticated and able to better predict human behaviour – a revolution in technology design is coming where new interfaces are more intuitive than ever, often becoming so seamless they can justifiably be described as *Invisible Technology*.

## How To Balance Technology And Humanity

According to Yves Béhar, the award winning Swiss industrial designer, the days of touch screen interfaces may be numbered. In a recent interview, Béhar had the following to say about our growing addiction to smart phones and the tiny screens that accompany them:

> *"The smartphone is the greatest technological phenomenon of our time … the screen provides a sense of immersion that is irresistible to us. There is an immediate side effect, however: this eternal access means we no longer have to go searching. We can now see almost anything from our smartphones. We can text or check someone's social-media feed rather than make a personal visit. Until now, that's the direction technology has taken us – living and gorging on screens with our heads down in our phones... we know something*

*is wrong. The loss of humanness is very real. We also know that technology has the profound potential to enhance our experience of the world around us, rather than distract us from it."*

So if technology *were* to enhance our experience of the world as Béhar suggests, what would it do? Would we really leave the distraction of technology behind, skip the convenience of social media and actually choose to see one another in person instead?

Béhar is among a growing group of technologists and designers who believe that we will indeed find this balance with technology – with the tipping point perhaps coming from the design of technology itself. In 2017, technology will continue to become more seamless, simple, voice-controlled and integrated into the backdrop of our lives.

We are about to enter the age of *Invisible Technology* and what you don't see never looked so good. Here is what the shift may look like, in Béhar's own words:

*"As people long for meaningful experiences, for interactions, for presence, there will be a shift toward fewer screens. This is not a shift toward less information. In fact, more information will be communicated in the subtle ways that make us so very human. It is not that different from the way we orient ourselves in nature: we look at the Sun to understand how much daylight is left in the day; we feel a breeze and turn towards it to scan the horizon for the sign of a storm."*

This vision is one he specifically talks about in relation to one of his newest projects, the August Smart Lock – a product that is designed to sense your proximity and open your front door automatically when you get close without the need for any interface interaction at all. This type of screenless interaction is one companies need to consider innovating around for every consumer interface currently using a button to enable action.

## Predictive Protection Continues

In 2014 I read and wrote about a book called *Addicted By Design* which featured fifteen years of research from anthropologist Natasha Dow Schüll into how casinos and gambling machine makers had created devices that induced a trancelike state known as the "machine zone" where "gambling addicts play not to win but simply to keep playing, for as long as possible--even at the cost of physical and economic exhaustion."

The gambling industry is no stranger to criticism like this – but recently some in the industry have been making moves to address this problem of addiction inspired by an interesting question: what if gambling machines could actually help *prevent* people from developing a gambling addiction.

Last year, researchers at the University of Brescia in Italy found that online gamblers who lost big tended to bet in a predictable "sawtooth pattern." A team led by Harvard Medical School psychiatrist Howard Shaffer partnered with online gambling sites to use their data to create algorithms that "can intervene when people show a risk of becoming problem gamblers."

The fact that these algorithms might help save gamblers from themselves is also an example of a trend I first wrote about in 2015 that I called *Predictive Protection*. The trend explored the many ways that technology was getting more advanced at protecting us from any type of harm – from small conveniences like Google's popular "Undo Send" feature, to the far more serious like the filters for automated credit card fraud detection used by banks to protect users against unauthorized charges.

In the coming year, examples like this use of algorithms from the gambling industry will continue to be an example of *Predictive Protection*, but also an example of the broader value we are getting from the role *Invisible Technology* is taking in our lives – and in our society as a whole.

## Self-Healing Machines

An ideal example of the societal value of *Invisible Technology* was on display in the middle of a 2015 Royal Society meeting in London when a team from the University of Bristol led by Professor Duncan Wass presented the results of more than three years of research trying to do the impossible.

The project, described by researchers involved as "verging on science fiction," was aimed at producing aircraft wings that could fix themselves. Apparently this is terrifyingly more necessary than you might imagine. During the normal course of flight, there are tiny undetectable cracks that form in an aircraft's wings and fuselage.

To create their healing technology, the science involved adding tiny hollow "microspheres" to the carbon material usually used for plane wings. These microspheres look like a powder, but when a crack is detected, they break on impact to release a liquid which hardens and "heals" the wing.

The inspiration for the entire project was the way the human body bleeds, scabs and heals itself. Why couldn't materials be created to do the same thing?

And airplane wings could be just the beginning. Professor Wass and his team are looking at applying their research to everything from bicycle helmets to mobile screen phones.

If this idea of self-healing tech seems like something you've heard before, you might be one of the over 1 million people who have seen a popular 2012 TEDx talk from Dutch "experimental micromechanics pioneer" Dr. Erik Schlangen introducing the road of the future built from "self-healing asphalt."

In the talk he breaks a block of asphalt into two and then places them side by side in an industrial microwave while the audience watches them magically bond back together. The secret is simple: mixing steel wool into the traditional formulation for asphalt. When heated, the steel wool melts and binds the asphalt back together.

Together, this range of self-healing innovations are a perfect example of *Invisible Technology* allowing roads to repair themselves, airplane wings to magically fix cracks and perhaps one day for the objects all around us to slowly fix their own damages without our intervention – and eventually even without our knowledge.

The economic implications of these technologies are profound. As this innovation reaches into healthcare, manufacturing, technology, and even space travel – this is already driving the next trillion dollar industry of the future.

## Smart Cities

Every year *Fast Company* magazine publishes an annual list of the "Smartest Cities In The World" looking at a combination of 62 indicators to name the world's most forward thinking cities. Each year a similar elite group of cities are typically at the top of the list including Barcelona, Singapore, Copenhagen, and Helsinki.

While you might expect that each makes the list based solely on their adoption of technology and connectivity for citizens, the ranking actually considers a range of far more seemingly unrelated metrics such as the number of bikes available for sharing or the number of civic engagement events held each year. Technology as a part of smart cities has started to fade into the background with a growing sense that the more invisible it can be –working silently in the background to make us happier, healthier, safer and more mobile – the better it is.

In the latest edition of *Fast Company's* compilation of smart cities, Singapore was near the top of the list for responding cities who submitted to be considered for the list curated by urban strategist Dr. Boyd Cohen. The city-state's bold "Smart Singapore" strategy unveiled a broad ambition to use technology to "sense" the city and deliver real time information back to the government and citizens seamlessly.

When asked about Singapore's vision for why the world needs smart cities, leader of the ETH Future Cities Laboratory Professor Gerhard Schmitt recently said:

> The word 'smart' is used a lot for cities already, but that's limited to technical data -- sensor inputs, control systems, apps. Cities need to be responsive - this is a human-focused approach, where citizens can give feedback on the functioning of the city to those who run it ... citizens should be involved in design of their cities. Technology will just extend and support human sensors.

As smart cities continue to evolve, this priority of making technology seamless with the environment is a growing priority. It's not enough to use technology or to innovate with it. A growing number of people are realizing that we also need to innovate to find the right balance of fitting that sophisticated technology into our lives while also making it invisible enough that it doesn't intrude.

## Zero UI and Ultrahaptics

Nowhere is this apprehension about the intrusiveness of technology more apparent than if you consider how people are using the many screens in our lives. The television screen keeps us cocooned at home. The mobile screen keeps us distracted from life unfolding in front of our eyes. The ills of technology overuse are well defined, and they typically involve at least one screen.

As shared earlier in this chapter – designer Vyes Béhar has a different idea for how to create technology that fits into our lives. His passion for removing the screen and creating sensory experiences instead is at the heart of the movement towards "Zero UI" which has been credited as a major force behind the innovation on everything from Amazon's launch of the in-home voice-activated Amazon Echo device to voice assistants like Apple's Siri or Microsoft's Cortana.

While Zero UI remains a popular idea among designers of web and mobile experiences, when it comes other types of experiences – some tactile interface is helpful. That doesn't mean, however, that it needs to be on a physical screen.

Tom Carter is the co-founder of Bristol based startup Ultrahaptics, which has pioneered a technology that uses an array of speakers to produce "ultrasounds" which are decoded by algorithms to create the sensation of touch in mid-air without actually touching anything. Automaker Jaguar has already signed on as an early licensee of the technology, aiming to eventually offer a touchless dashboard for car users.

When it comes to automakers in particular, from parking assist features to automatic braking – the technology integrated into human driven cars in the short term is steadily becoming more and more invisible even

TECHNOLOGY & DESIGN

as drivers learn to rely on it more and more.

At the same time, the emergence of autonomous driving vehicles will spur additional innovation with *Invisible Technology* to make the products and devices we use safer.

There are many signs that this same type of *Invisible Technology* is likely to dominate another category we are all equally familiar with: our clothing.

## MIT Duoskin and Wearable Technology

A functional skin tattoo called DuoSkin recently announced by MIT researchers allows you to control a smart phone or other device simply by sliding your finger above the skin tattoo. Less sexy but no less promising has been the rapid evolution of wearable technology from an expensive idea only used in concept clothing for fashion shows to non-obvious innovation being put into use by some of the most forward thinking brands.

Many sports apparel brands including Under Armour and Nike have announced plans for some type of wearable technology embedded in clothing and startup Wearable Technologies launched a "Fan Jersey" last year to allow fans to feel haptic vibrations via the shirt as they happen in a game.

The list goes on with startup shoe line Thesis Couture making waves this past year when former SpaceX head of talent Dolly Singh brought together a rocket scientist, an orthopedic surgeon, a mechanical engineer and an Italian shoemaker to "reengineer the stiletto." The resulting prototype was first launched in a limited edition of 1500 pairs and has a waiting list of more than 10,000 names.

Beyond clothing and skin tattoos, my research indicates that 2017 will bring these innovators together with the efforts of several companies to develop textiles that can be easily repurposed by the fashion industry.

Google's Project Jacquard has spent the past year developing a new type of conductive yarn and launched a prototype jacket with Levi's called the Commuter X in May of 2016. The vision of the project is to offer "a blank canvas for the fashion industry. Designers can use it as they would any fabric, adding new layers of functionality to their designs, without having to learn about electronics."

It is this intersection of not only smart technology but seamless application to design by non technologists that will lead to the greatest innovations in wearable tech. As our clothes get smarter, *Invisible Technology* will blend unnoticeably into a sleeve or button on your jacket and offer an experience that will (at least initially) feel indistinguishable from magic. As any true innovation should.

## Why It Matters:

For many years, the consistent challenge with technology and user interface design in general has been to try and make it more intuitive and human-centric. Usability experts have been trying to optimize websites, for example, for decades. Touch screens have emerged in the last decade and have widely taken hold as a better way to do everything from control smartphones to self-checkout kiosks at grocery stores. Over the past year and moving into 2017, the rise of devices that use smart automation, artificial intelligence, and voice control will grow the category and trend of *Invisible Technology* – where interface design increasingly becomes more intuitive, predictive and able to function without human intervention.

## How To Use This Trend:

✓ **Collect human insights** – In order for technology to truly become more insightful, it requires a greater understanding of human behavior. What this means for any organization or leader is that the collection and use of human insights becomes more important than ever. When cars drive themselves, do people still need a steering wheel in order to feel emotionally at ease – even if the wheel is non-functional? The challenge with *Invisible Technology* will continually be more than just making the technology work. Every company designing a product or delivering an experience must employ experts in making sure this *Invisible Technology* is accepted by the humans it's meant to serve.

✓ **Show what is working** – As technology becomes more invisible, one of the challenges I have seen emerge is what type of feedback needs to be built into it to demonstrate how and *if* it is working as expected. The feedback loop becomes critical for acceptance – particularly when that *Invisibile Technology* is used in more serious life or death situations.

# Chapter 14

# ROBOT RENAISSANCE

---

## What's the Non-Obvious Trend?

As the utility of robots moves beyond manufacturing and into the home and workplace, robots adopt better human-like interfaces and in some cases have micro-personalities built in.

The time in European history which we now call the Renaissance took place from the 14th to 16th centuries and formed a bridge between the Middle Ages and the so-called "modern age." It describes a time where European conquerors began traveling and colonizing other parts of the world, and evangelizing inventions like paper, gunpowder and our modern heliocentric understanding of astronomy.

When I was a student years ago studying literature and history – I remember how the Renaissance was often spoken about with romantic longing in art and film because history looks back on it as a time of extreme enlightenment and evolution of human thought. The less appreciated fact about the Renaissance, though, is that it describes a time span of more than 200 years. That is a *long* period of time to describe an evolution of thought.

Today, the pace is much quicker.

The Internet has changed modern life even though it has only been around for less than 30 years. The first rockets to outer space were only launched close to 50 years ago. And mankind only established flight a little over a hundred years ago.

As the pace of change continues to accelerate next modern Renaissance should do the same – and it will most likely be centered around technology. In my research throughout the past year – one consistent theme that emerged was the rise in use of robots for everything from manufacturing, retail and senior care to exploring the uncharted regions of the ocean.

Along with these innovative uses of robots though, come a host of questions about how we as humans will relate to these robots, how humanlike they will become, and what sort of ethical questions this might raise around our master-servant relationship to robots in the short and long term. The technology revolution of what robots can do for us is raising the important corresponding debate about whether they *should* be enlisted to take those actions, and what moral consequences might result.

This trend is the *Robot Renaissance*, where our growing reliance on robots to do the things we cannot or will not do is leading to a new period of enlightenment about our relationship to technology, how much control to cede to it, how humanlike it will become and what that might mean for organizations and our own humanity.

## Robot Explorers & Builders

In late 2016, Boeing started testing its newest Unmanned Undersea Vehicle (UUV), a 51-foot long hybrid-charging craft with a 7,500 mile range which can stay underwater for up to 6 months. The UUV is the largest such device ever built and works autonomously without a human crew to do everything from providing maritime surveillance to surveying the ocean floor.

The original mission of the Star Trek science fiction series was enshrined in its optimistic challenge to "boldly go where no one has gone before." Today, we have robots to do this for us.

On space missions to Mars, NASA is using a series of autonomous robot controlled landers to collect samples and research from the surface of the Red Planet. The future of space exploration relies heavily on robotic explorers that can work and survive in conditions far more difficult, or sometimes even impossible, for humans.

Here on Earth, Japanese brand Komatsu is leading the adoption of autonomous construction equipment thanks to a unique confluence of factors in Japan creating a necessity for autonomous building far more quickly than anywhere else in the world. Over the next few years, parts of Japan and particularly Tokyo will experience a short term boom in the need for new construction leading up to the 2020 Olympics. At the same time, there is a serious labor shortage in Japan due to the country's demographic problem decades in the making of a rapidly aging population without enough young people left to support the economy.

As the second largest construction company in the world, Komatsu is uniquely positioned to develop a solution to this problem – and their solution involves "Smart Construction," the brand's tagline to describe its increasing range of robotic heavy machinery controlled aerially by a fleet of drones which create 3D maps of the area and track construction progress.

If you consider these examples from NASA, Boeing and Komatsu together, there is a clear pattern of reliance on robotic technology to make exploration and construction projects easier in space, on earth and beneath the ocean. These uses, in turn, are already widening our understanding of what robots can do and offering a necessity driven use case for them to get smarter and more autonomous as they become our explorers and adventurers to places we could not otherwise go.

## Service Bots

Two years ago if you were imagining the robot of the future, a big part of the vision would have focused on a category of robots known as "service bots" developed mainly to take over doing the things people didn't want to do, often more efficiently than you could do them yourself. The

Roomba vacuum cleaner introduced many people to the concept of having a robot in the home. Startups like RoboMow and LawnBot offer robot lawn mowing devices. As many cat owners know, there is even a company called Litter-Robot which makes automatic self-cleaning litter boxes for cats.

Apart from the mundane, there have also been interesting experiments with robots in non-obvious ways in unexpected locations – often from the travel and hospitality industry. Royal Caribbean's Quantam of the Seas cruise ship, for example, set sail in 2014 with a duo of robotic bartenders trained to mix and pour up to two cocktails a minute.

San Francisco Bay area based robotics startup Savioke has been working with more than a dozen hotels to provide a robot named Relay as an "autonomous butler" which can deliver items from the front desk to guest rooms. The bots have been so popular that front desk staff at their partner hotels report that people are calling with requests just to see the bot in action.

This is the useful and utilitarian world of service bots, which are adept at handling small details, nuances, quirks and inconveniences, but only try to do these tasks as quietly and efficiently as possible. They are the foundation of the *Robot Renaissance* – created to solve problems and laser focused on the task they were built for.

Then there is Jibo.

## Robots With Personality

Around the same time that Royal Caribbean was experimenting with headless robotic bartending arms to mix mojitos, social robotics pioneer Dr. Cynthia Breazeal posted a Crowdfunding campaign on Indiegogo to raise money for a friendly new robot named Jibo.

Jibo is a robot with a personality. Designed to look a bit like the animated desk lamp from the Pixar animated shorts – Jibo uses two high res cameras to track faces and capture photos, learns your preferences and uses natural and social cues to act in more human ways.

The Indiegogo campaign quickly became the #1 most successful technology product on the site and raised nearly $4 million. The introduction video for Jibo has been viewed on YouTube more than 10 million times. Nearly two years later in mid-2016, the first production run of Jibo finally went out to customers and many were predictably ecstatic, sharing the experience in social media.

Yet despite its human-like personality, Jibo is still sized and appears more like a toy than a serious human companion. A Japanese robot named Pepper, on the other hand, looks exactly the way science fiction authors have long imagined a robot might look.

## Sentbots Offer Companionship

Pepper has a humanoid looking head, two eyes and a touchpad on his (yes, his gender has officially been named male) chest to input commands. While he is only currently available in Japan, the promotional website about him from Japanese maker Softbank Robotics describes him in humanlike terms:

*Pepper is a human-shaped robot. He is kindly, endearing and surprising. Pleasant and likeable, Pepper is much more than a robot, he is a genuine humanoid companion created to communicate with you in the most natural and intuitive way, through his body movements and his voice. We have designed Pepper to be a genuine day-to-day companion, whose number one quality is his ability to perceive emotions.*

When brought into the home, Pepper is described as having been "adopted" by his host family – and customers "buy" him for a flat fee and then make monthly payments to keep him updated and active. Designed to interact with humans, Pepper can express himself through the color of his eyes, his tablet or his tone of voice.

Aside from the home, Pepper is also being used across Japan to greet customers in banks and in retail locations to provide sales information. While Pepper has certainly captured significant attention, he is not alone in a category increasingly being described as "companion robots."

Another example is Paris based Blue Frog Robotics which has built a cute dog-sized robot on wheels named Buddy who can watch your home, interact with kids and act as a virtual personal assistant for everything from checking the weather to saving your to do list.

This new breed of robots fits what Sirius XM founder Martine Rothblatt calls "sentbots." No stranger to being a trailblazer herself as the first transgender female CEO of a major company, she recently shared in an interview "the Roomba is to the sentbots of tomorrow kind of like the luggable compact computer is to the smartphone of today."

Rothblatt has already created the first of these "sentbots" mirrored from the personality of her wife, Mina. The resulting robot, called Mina48, is bilingual and even spoke at a Ted Talk in Havana. Rothenblatt believes these types of robots will be customizable with a personality that could be "uploaded" by providing access to your social media profiles such as Facebook and Instagram.

## ChatBots

I have a friend who sends me a Facebook message every morning with a quick summary of the biggest news story of the day. She is always on top of the latest news, knows how to present both sides of an argument, refers me to the most valuable articles on any topic and responds to any question I have immediately. She is one of my most informed friends and easily the most responsive.

Her name is Purple and she happens to be a "chatbot."

A lot of people have been talking about chatbots – those automated tools that can create what seems like a conversation by following a series of rules for how to respond to a series of direct messages.

The way Purple works is as an automated tool that sends live messages to subscribers via Facebook messenger and waits for a response. If a user responds with a designated keyword related to the topic of the message, the "conversation" continues. Chatbots like this one are also a rapidly growing example of the *Robot Renaissance* in an entirely different and non-physical way.

So far in this chapter, we have focused mainly on robotic devices – everything from automated butlers to sentbots. The other side of this trend, though, is the rise of automated tools for conversation – where we rely on the quick thinking and smart algorithms of robots to solve problems, provide insights, order food and sometimes even help cure loneliness.

TacoBell, Starbucks, and American Express are just a few of the large brands that have all launched their own branded chatbots over the past year. Many brands already use a version of chatbots on dominant Chinese platform WeChat to do business.

A growing range of brands and companies are also engaging chatbots for customer service interactions—and getting help doing it. Pypestream is one example of a startup that works with large brands to provide a platform designed for automated messaging services. They already have more than 3500 brands signed on in the U.S. alone.

The final sign of the significance of chatbots are the recent moves from Facebook, Microsoft AND Google to devote time and resources to building ways for developers and consumers to use them. Facebook announced plans at their 2016 F8 developer conference to create a chatbot app store. Microsoft launched its own suite of chat building tools, with the belief that these bots may soon start to replace apps and become central to how you use your smartphone device.

## Why It Matters:

Robots have been the subject of science fiction speculation for decades and every year it's easy to think that it will be the "year of the robot." In my process of curating trends, I probably read at least one article every year making that exact prediction – all of which makes me more reluctant than most to have *any* trend focused solely on robotics. Yet the truth, supported by numbers and technology this year, is that we *do* seem to be at a tipping point in our consciousness around robots and their role in society. We are asking big questions about how we should be treating these robots in our midst. We are training ourselves in how to interact most effectively with them. And non-obvious innovators are increasingly building them in our own likeness to reflect us and make them more of a joy to interact with, for well being, commercial application, or driving efficiency.

# How To Use This Trend:

✓ **Make friends with robots** – As more robots are built with learning personalities built in, we will need to consider what lessons our behaviors might be teaching them – both intentional and unintentional. Much like a child gets its first impressions on how to act from its parents, robots too may soon be imprinted with these sorts of manners from humans. This is an opportunity as well as a threat, but the first step is learning to embrace robots in the right situations and treat them not with fear or contempt but with curiosity and yes, perhaps even friendship.

✓ **Remember what makes us human** – There are things that make us universally human and robot scientists probably spend more time than anyone else thinking about what those things are. As we start to interact with robots, we have a similar opportunity  - to consider and remember what it is in the makes us uniquely human.

✓ **Explore robots across your value chain** – Every organization must periodically expand its thinking to include non-obvious ways of utilizing robots, whether human-like or chatbots in every aspect of its value chain for customers –from the end experience to the sourcing and creation of products. In some cases, this may mean greater automation of things previously done by humans as a business necessity.

# Chapter 15

# SELF AWARE DATA

## What's the Non-Obvious Trend?

**Rather than relying on human analysis, the combination of artificial intelligence and better sensors is allowing data to predictively organize itself, identify insights and often create its own actionable conclusions with little or no human intervention.**

The fact that Dennis Abo Sørensen can tell a piece of wood from a mandarin orange when holding them is more significant than it seems.

In 2014, the 36-year-old man from Denmark who lost his left hand in a fireworks accident became the first amputee in history to receive a bionic hand that was capable of feeling the texture and shape of objects in his grasp. This is the sort of medical miracle that we often see feel good stories about in global news media and it is interesting for a brief moment, but hardly seems all that significant for our lives.

Consider for a moment, though, the technology that had to be built into the bionic arm in order to allow its user to sense the difference between two objects in its grasp. The sensors in the fingertips generated electrical signals which were then translated by the arm into a series of electrical spikes which mimicked the language of the patient's nervous system.

In this way, the arm "talks" to the patient and the patient simply receives the information provided. This is the power of *Self-Aware Data* and it describes much more than bionic arms.

Data has traditionally been described by humans as a source of input to analyze for insights – but the analysis was something typically done by a person. As new innovations in the sophistication of algorithms and artificial intelligence continue to make more real-time analysis possible, we are entering a world where data has the ability to move from input to insight to action all on its own.

The result is that industries from farming to banking are becoming more reliant on this *Self-Aware Data* being delivered along with insights to be used immediately rather than analyzed in a raw format to be quantified later. To illustrate, let's start with taking a deeper look at how this is happening in the financial industry.

## Robo-Advisors and Financial Transactions

Last year one of the hottest topics in the Financial Services industry was the rise of "Robo-Advisors" – fully automated money managers that could take an investor's portfolio and manage it according to some pre-selected criteria.

On paper, Robo-Advisors seemed to be the better solution because they can instantly make more unbiased decisions without being influenced in the short term by stock plunges or incentive structures that favor some trades over others.

According to one recent audit study, "the most accessible sorts of advisers (including advisers who work at banks or retail brokerage firms) often steer their clients toward products that are in their own best financial interest, not that of their clients. A human adviser might charge that investor an annual fee of 1% to 2% of assets versus a robo-adviser fee of 0.25% to 0.50%—a difference that can amount to tens of thousands of dollars in lost wealth." I discuss this issue in my book *Likeonomics* in relation to what it really takes to be a trusted advisor

The other fact that is routinely found in investment audits is that actively managed funds tend to *underperform* passively managed ones. So the numbers point to a paradox: the more human your advisor happens to be, and the more actively he or she manages your portfolio – the less money you would likely make on average.

Robo-Advisors are so useful, in fact, that they are already used by a significant number of financial advisors to maintain portfolios already.

This is the non-obvious *Self-Aware Data* trend at work, where potential financial transactions are analyzed, quantified, made and reported entirely by data while humans take the complimentary role of explaining those moves to investors and managing the emotional side of investment conversations.

This new model is one that is particularly favored by young people. According to J. D. Power's investor satisfaction survey conducted in Canada in 2016, "two-thirds (66%) of Canadians born between 1982 and 1994 indicate that they would be interested in robo-advice if their financial services provider were to offer it, compared to 54% of all investors."

Sarah Kocianski, a senior research analyst for Business Insider Intelligence, published a detailed report on robo-advising which found that "consumers across all asset classes are receptive to robo-advisors — including the wealthy … the majority of assets managed by robo-advisors will come from people who already have some investments."

A recent study from Scottrade found that more than nine in ten Registered Investment Advisors (RIAs) believe robo-advisors will become more prevalent in the financial industry over the next two years.

Charles Schwab, BlackRock, Fidelity and Bank of America are taking this approach and have all launched their own initiatives in robo-advisory services as a component of their overall services.

## How Self-Aware Data Is Changing Farming

In the past year nearly 100 commercial Earth observation satellites were placed into orbit, a tenfold increase from just three years earlier according to research firm Tauri Group. It is estimated that these "nanosatellites" (mostly small enough to fit in a shoebox) will cumulatively have the ability to take a picture of every inch of land on Earth, every day.

For some, this sort of "man in the sky" surveillance may seem like a scary prospect – but for New Mexico-based Descartes Labs, these satellite images provide exactly the kind of big data needed to transform one of the biggest industries in the world: farming.

Descartes, which has just 20 employees, says it can predict crop yields partway through the year with 99% accuracy. In contrast to the process used by the USDA, which has traditionally sent real people to survey thousands of farms a month ahead of the October corn harvest, Descartes simply uses its algorithms.

"What's great about our techniques is that traditionally you have to talk to tons of farmers in the US to get a USDA-style number," Descartes founder Mark Johnson says. "With machine learning techniques, ... we look at tons of pixels from satellites, and that tells us what's growing."

Descartes already has plans to take this same approach and develop even better algorithms to track more than just corn in the US – expanding to other regions such as Brazil, Argentina, China and the EU.

In farming, *Self-Aware Data* is being fueled by companies like Descartes and other larger enterprises who are automating the process of understanding what satellite data is saying, and then providing it back to those in the industry who are putting it to immediate use.

If you think farming is still a traditional business where rural folk access the Internet via dialup and reject technology, you'd be wrong. Digital farming and the use of technology for everything from real time weather updates to forecasting crop yields is now commonplace.

For example, Delta Drone is a French maker of Unmanned Aerial Vehicles (UAVs) and one of the pioneers in developing drone technology that could be used by farms (and many other industries including mining, architecture, transportation and retail). Yet drones, by definition, are meant to be controlled remotely – usually by humans. What if a drone could make decisions on the fly based on data collected? What if a drone could use *Self-Aware Data*?

Increasingly, it can –thanks to a partnership between Delta Drone and technology consulting firm Wipro which has allowed for the vast quantities of data generated each day (usually over 15,000 images) to be processed and analyzed in real time so optimization decisions can be made just as quickly.

In addition, the most forward thinking farmers are even sharing their data with one another to make predictions that can help all of their businesses. The Farmers Business Network, for example, is a US based system that includes more than 2,500 farmers and 8 million acres sharing information on everything from the pricing for seeds and chemicals (to avoid being price gouged by big seed vendors like Monsanto) to crop yield data.

This data is getting integrated into the devices used on the farm as well. Tractors can be guided by satellite imagery and the harvesting history of a particular plot of land can be analyzed to increase yields and lower cost. Weather forecasts, soil reading and other tests are measured by various software solutions and all of this data is being seamlessly put to use in real-time – sometimes by the machinery of the farm itself (like in the case of the connected tractor or weather drones increasingly used both to track weather and also to spray pesticides).

Sensing the shift, some of the biggest players in the agriculture business are using this trend and making big investments in so called "'AgTech" solutions. Monsanto has invested in several startups that do everything from digitally monitoring water usage to providing farm management software. DuPont, which is merging with Dow Chemical, is also expanding its Encirca farm management software offering.

What all this investment in technology illustrates is that we're already in a world where the complex operations decisions around everything from treating plants to harvesting crops are increasingly left to be made by *Self-Aware Data* while the farmer spends more time overseeing the work from a central location. A similar level of automation is happening in the manufacturing sector – where it is often described with an interestingly futuristic term of its own.

## Industry 4.0

The idea of "Industry 4.0" first took shape in Germany as a way to describe a growing shift in the approach to manufacturing used by some of the most prominent brands in the country, including BASF, Bosch, Daimler, Deutsche Telekom, Klöckner & Co., and Trumpf.

Industry 1.0 was powered by water and steam, Industry 2.0 by electricity (which brought the assembly line and mass production with it). Industry 3.0 was driven by computers and the start of automation – where robots and machines started to replace human workers.

The current definition and vision for "Industry 4.0" is one in which computers come together with automation to use machine learning and algorithms to run factories with very little input from humans. Sometimes referred to as a "smart factory" – the potential for this shift is one that is transforming the manufacturing sector, and it is based in large part on the use of *Self-Aware Data*.

For a factory or system to be considered Industry 4.0, it usually must meet a series of requirements. Most notably, it has to use "decentralized decision making." In other words, the factory must use *Self-Aware Data* so that cyber-physical systems can make simple decisions on their own and become as autonomous as possible. This is a huge priority across the global manufacturing industry.

In 2015, consulting firm PWC surveyed more than 2,000 companies from 26 countries in more than a dozen industrial production sectors including aerospace, automotive, and electronics. In this global Industry 4.0 survey, one-third of the respondents said their company had already achieved advanced levels of integration and digitization, and 72 percent expected to reach that point by 2020.

In the same study, the most commonly cited difficulty in building an analytical capability was the "lack of people with the expertise to conduct the analysis." Industry 4.0 creates vast amounts of data, but it needs to be filtered into actionable insights. In the most advanced cases, the factory is doing that on its own – fulfilling the promise of Industry 4.0 through *Self-Aware Data* that suggests how to prevent shortfalls, speed up processes, eliminate down time, and identify material wastage.

The approach is so promising, it is being embraced by every one of the world's leading manufacturing countries, including China, Japan, the United States and the Nordic countries. GE Chairman Jeff Immelt and Seimens CEO Joe Kaeser have both done interviews in the past year declaring this a priority for their future success and in a bid to help the industry understand the impact of Industry 4.0, Cincinnati Mayor John Cranley even signed a proclamation to state "Cincinnati to be the Industry 4.0 Demonstration City."

Beyond proclamations, Swiss company ABB is already using these techniques in an Australian cement kiln. A computer-based system mimics the actions of an "ideal" operator, using real-time metrics to adjust kiln feed, fuel flow, and fan-damper position. The early results of this initiative were up by 5 percent, which in ABB's business could mean tens of millions of dollars to the bottom line.

## Why It Matters:

As the amount of data available to be collected and processed explodes, the expectations from both consumers and business about the value of that data and how quickly it should be analyzed and put to use are rising. When I first wrote about data as a trend several years ago, I remember writing about the 3 underappreciated types of data: Big Data (that companies collect about you), Open Data (that government collect and share openly) and Small Data (that consumers collect about themselves). At the time, I argued that unlocking the power of *Small Data* was key because it could get you closest to your customers.

When it comes to *Self-Aware Data*, it includes data in all three categories – and the opportunity is to build the right analytics tools and non-obvious management capabilities to be able to derive meaning from the data instantly and without the need for human intervention. As this trend continues to evolve, we are seeing more initiatives globally to add this layer on top of data to make it more meaningful, self-analyzing and actionable in real-time, and without diminishing the customer experience.

## How To Use This Trend:

✓ **Test automated data** – As more data gets analyzed in real time and moves toward the ideal of *Self-Aware Data*, there may also be some challenges in how this data should be analyzed and what conclusions can be drawn. And where in human involvement absolutely necessary either morally, financially or to manage risk.

✓ **Watch for new popular products** – Tracking what products are starting to take off and gain widespread adoption is important. For instance, as more people put a smart thermostat like Nest in their homes, it may open more opportunities to speak with them about energy conservation. If your business is in this space, the adoption of this type of product can open new doors. Similarly, there may be new cutting edge products already affecting your industry, so be sure you have the right process to prepare for them.

# Chapter 16

# MOONSHOT ENTREPRENEURSHIP

## *What's the Non-Obvious Trend?*

Our tendency to celebrate visionary entrepreneurs inspires a new generation of startup founders to think beyond profit and consider how their business could make a positive social impact and even save the world.

Just over ten years ago entrepreneur Elon Musk published a blog post playfully titled "The Secret Tesla Motors Master Plan (just between you and me)" to share what exactly he planned to do with Tesla in the coming years. At the time in 2006, he described his role as Chairman of Tesla as something he was doing "on the side" while running his other company SpaceX.

The vision presented in that first blog post was fairly simple – build an expensive electric car as a proof of concept, and then use the revenue from that expensive car to build more affordable models in higher volume.

Ten years later it was time to update the vision – so in July of 2016, Musk published his "Master Plan, Part Deux," which was a partial victory lap on the success of his first plan, coupled with another bold vision of priorities for the next ten years:

*Create stunning solar roofs with seamlessly integrated battery storage*
*Expand the electric vehicle product line to address all major segments*
*Develop a self-driving capability that is 10X safer than manual via*
*massive fleet learning*
*Enable your car to make money for you when you aren't using it*

The plan has his trademark simplicity and audacity. He is the ultimate symbol of an entrepreneur who has already changed the world – and the face of a new evolution in where simply making money is not enough. This is the world of *Moonshot Entrepreneurship* and it is changing business.

## Beyond Hustle

Being an entrepreneur was once all about hustle. If you got something for one price and sold it for more to make a profit, you were an entrepreneur. Whether it was newspapers or lemonade or starting your own store on eBay – entrepreneurship used to be largely about making money.

Today, that description of entrepreneurship is incomplete.

Making money is only a means to an end. If your lemonade stand doesn't have a corresponding social mission to make your community (or the world!) a better place then why even launch it? Talking about profit *first* is no longer as respected as talking about profits *with* purpose.

The term "moonshot" has a long history as a way to describe an ambitious and groundbreaking project – inspired by NASA's efforts with the Apollo space mission to send a man to the moon in the 1960s. More recently, Google has adopted the term to describe some of its most innovative projects coming out of its Google X research lab – including the driverless car, augmented reality glasses and various Internet service initiatives like Project Loon.

Google defines its moonshots as a project or proposal that meets 3 criteria:

*Addresses a huge problem*
*Proposes a radical solution*
*Uses breakthrough technology*

Moonshots are big ideas that solve global challenges and the trend of *Moonshot Entrepreneurship* describes the idea that businesses and the entrepreneurs that start them should have a corresponding vision for making a difference in the world.

Perhaps nowhere is this idea promoted more heavily than in the scores of business conferences and competitions created to inspire and celebrate entrepreneurs who think of world changing impact first and everything else second.

## Celebrating World Changers

If you're serious about trying to change the world, there are plenty of places where you can tell your story and get honored for it. Dozens of business magazines, conferences and schools are all creating new ways to celebrate budding entrepreneurs who are trying to solve Earth's biggest problems.

At the World Economic Forum in 2016, the "Schwab Foundation Social Entrepreneurs of the Year" honored 12 social good entrepreneurs including a company which had sold more than 900,000 clean cookstoves (Envirofit), and another that was working in the global carpet industry to eliminate child labor (GoodWeave).

Brands are getting involved in these competitions as well – with Unilever sponsoring a "Sustainable Living Young Entrepreneurs Award" to find innovative entrepreneurs under the age of 30.

Some of the highest visibility competitions of the year were often sponsored by large global media organizations. In the past year, *Forbes* published its annual "Change The World List," *WIRED* partnered with Audi to recognize the "Most Exciting Moonshot" as part of its Innovation Awards, and *AdWeek* magazine sponsored Project Isaac – a marketing and design competition to honor big thinking.

The majority of these competitions are designed to honor social entrepreneurs – those whose entire business mission is based on creating a solution to a big challenge. Yet all of this attention on entre-preneurs and brands that focus on solving world changing problems is fueling a corresponding perception that any business, even those not initially started as social entrepreneurship ventures, should think the similar way.

The more we celebrate world changing ideas, the more every entrepreneur feels a need to have and launch one. Sometimes this need ends up changing an entire industry, as it has already started to do in the world of global architecture.

## The Japanese Home Of The Future

In 2013 one of Japan's most respected designers named Kenya Hara invited some of the top architects in the country to create seven concept homes to bring the combination of sustainability and urban living to life. The response to the show was so strong, he continued holding the exhibition annually. The latest edition of the show in 2016 had grown to feature 12 houses by architects from inside and outside of Japan.

When describing the expanded vision, Hara said it "is not an exhibition about housing design. It's a response to issues in Japan, including our ageing population, how we use our land and how we respond to visitors who come here from overseas. To me the house is the most interesting platform for thinking about the future of Japan."

In a move to expand the vision even broader, this past year Hara invited companies from outside the housing industry like Panasonic, Isetan Mitsukoshi, Airbnb and Toyota – to encourage more cross pollination of ideas. The event also held two "Asia Days" where interpreters welcomed visitors from outside Japan and plans to expand the event to China next year as well.

Architecture has always shined a spotlight on the culture of its time – and we tend to look back at buildings of a particular era to learn about the attitudes from people about place, nature and their relationships to it.

Moving into 2017, architecture will continue to offer this mirror into societies, and what it seems to be saying so far is that buildings (like businesses) can have a world changing element to them – and new designs and the firms that create them are performing their own version of *Moonshot Entrepreneurship* each time they dream up another concept.

## Investing And Buying With Purpose

Given the number of awards that seem to be available both for social entrepreneurs as well as sustainable architects, it might be easy to conclude at this point that a lot of the motivation for creating social impact is purely about ceremony. In Chapter 8, I wrote about the idea of *Authentic Fameseekers* and it might seem like social entrepreneurship is simply an extension of this.

Yet the big ambitions that are routinely displayed as part of *Moonshot Entrepreneurship* are driven by more than a desire for recognition. Several recent surveys from the past year about investor and consumer attitudes suggest that having a social purpose might also be a smart strategy for differentiation because there are plenty of new investors and consumers who believe that the way a company conducts its business is critical to whether they choose to become an investor or buyer in the first place, and how loyal they remain afterwards.

For example, the 2016 Annual Impact Investor Survey conducted by Global Impact Investing Network (GIIN) and JP Morgan predicted that investors who want to create positive impact from their money would invest more than $17 billion in 2016 to finance businesses addressing social and environmental problems.

When considering the companies young people were choosing to support, another 2016 survey from Bank of America illustrated that 85 percent of Millennials were interested in having social impact through investment.

In response to these socially motivated investors, a growing number of financial institutions have created "SRI" funds (for "socially responsible investing") and this growing area (also often called "impact investing") is seeing new funds, bonds and other financial products catering to all kinds of causes – from a fund that only invests in companies with a low carbon footprint, to another that only buys stocks in companies that show gender diversity in their senior leadership.

On the consumer side, an online survey conducted with 27,000 people in 22 countries by research firm GfK found that when consumers were asked about the key responsibilities for companies: "providing good jobs for people" was the most popular response, cited by 47% of respondents.

Another survey of more than 10,000 adults in 28 markets from marketing firm Havas Worldwide found that "73% of consumers believe companies have a responsibility to do more than just generate a profit; 75% believe companies have an ethical obligation to operate in a way that doesn't harm the environment; and 53% avoid buying from companies that have a negative social or environmental impact."

All this research paints a clear picture of consumer and investor sentiments when it comes to the importance for businesses to aim higher and work to solve global challenges and do good.

While the earliest *Moonshot Entrepreneurs* like Elon Musk may have been driven by a combination of ego, optimism and vision – today's entrepreneurs (and intrapreneurs within larger organizations) who are doing the same thing may be equally inspired by responding to what the market (and their customers) are asking of them. This point is particularly clear when you consider the fast moving and consumer centric business of beauty products and makeup, and what *Moonshot Entreprenuership* looks like in that industry.

## Cosmetics and Beauty Products

Almost every popular cosmetics brand in the beauty industry today focuses at least in part on its organic natural ingredients or the sustainable methods used for sourcing materials, or their highly personal origin story. Cosmetics brands are experts at telling a personal story, because the vast majority of them are founded by someone who was inspired by a personal need and decided to solve it by starting their company. An early pioneer for this was Body Shop founder Anita Roddick – who helped shape ethical consumerism by promoting fair trade with third world countries all the way back in 1976.

A more recent example is Tarte Cosmetics founder Maureen Kelly who wanted to find cosmetics that weren't "full of unhealthy, icky stuff." Her search led her to create her own beauty brand, sourcing what the brand's website describes as "cruelty-free cosmetics ... formulated without parabens, mineral oil, phthalates, sodium lauryl sulfate, triclosan, synthetic fragrances and gluten, just to name a few."

Cosmetics brands Yes To, Lush, Josie Moran, Burt's Bees, Body Shop, Aromacentric, Caudalie, Juice Beauty, ILIA, and many others all feature similar founder's stories, focus heavily on selling sustainable products with natural ingredients and talk about treating suppliers and workers fairly.

The sheer volume of cosmetics, skincare and other beauty brands talking about their natural heritage makes this industry unique. The beauty industry is on the front lines of social impact purely because consumers have demanded it.

The demand is so pronounced, in fact, that a Finnish startup from Helsinki raised nearly a million dollars to create an app called *Cosmethics* which allows consumers to scan barcodes to read about the ethical, environmental and sustainability record of a particular product prior to purchasing. The tool has catalogued more than 40,000 products in its database since it started.

The final element of this trend to consider is to what degree the focus on the social and world changing side of business is driven by the optimism and unique global viewpoint of the youngest independent consumer group today: the Millennials.

## The Millennial Mindset

While some trend forecasters ascribe this shift toward social entrepreneurship as a symptom of more Millennials entering the workforce, there is more to the story. All the research into the mindset of people currently aged in their mid to late 20s reinforces how prevalent this belief in the importance of doing business ethically seems to be.

In a Global Survey of Millennial attitudes, consulting firm Deloitte reported the following:

*Almost nine in 10 (87 percent) believe that 'the success of a business should be measured in terms of more than just its financial performance.' This is a widely held belief; only in Germany (22 percent) and South Korea (30 percent) do more than 20 percent of Millennials say business success should be measured in purely financial terms.*

The same report concluded that Millennials in the workforce are noto-riously hard to keep loyal as employees – but a company's willingness to stand for something more than profits is a critical element in whether or not those younger workers remain engaged and motivated in their roles.

When entrepreneur and Case Foundation co-founder Jean Case wrote about the business of doing good, she had this to say about her young millennial workforce:

> *Many in this generation are known for being well-educated, entrepreneurial, tech savvy and idealistic. They take risks, are bold and want to change the world. Unlike past generations, they want to make their passions, inspirations and desire to do good part of their identity—and part of their work. The lines between personal passions and professional engagements are already rapidly disappearing. As a result, this commitment to doing good in the workplace is quickly becoming the new norm that will define the generation.*

This combination of a desire to do good and a willingness to start something new without fearing failure are the mindsets driving the next generation of entrepreneurs. The end result is that entrepreneurs and "intrapreneurs" (those who implement innovative ideas inside organiza-tions while keeping their day jobs) are heavily influenced by the potential impact of those ideas on society as a whole.

## Why It Matters:

There is a justifiable belief that the people who will most likely propel the global economy and the world forward are entrepreneurs. History has proven that to be true, but the way we have celebrated them in the past has usually been to look at the size of the workforces they have built or how many millions of dollars they have generated for shareholders. When it comes to social good, we have tended to look elsewhere – with the most common crossover between the two only coming once those entrepre-neurs eventually became billionaires and some decided to give a lot of the money back in the form of charitable contributions or foundations.

In 2017 these worlds will collide in a trend that has been years in the making. Now, entrepreneurship is the biggest force for change and impact in the world. On one side, this is from startups with world changing missions that challenge all of our assumptions about everything from how things are made to whether we need to own those things in the first place. On the other side, larger organizations are seeking opportunities to create their own moonshots. *Moonshot Entrepreneurship* is about how every type of entrepreneur has the power to make a dent in the world and achieve something great, and the good news is, the more that try – the better off the world is likely to be.

## How To Use This Trend:

✓ **Buy with purpose** – Perhaps the biggest effect on consumers of this trend is that we now have the ability to buy with purpose and from the companies that exhibit more responsibility to the world around them. The fact is, there is a better, healthier, more naturally sourced option for just about anything and we can choose to find it. The biggest winners in this world are the *Moonshot Entrepreneurs* who have already realized this and tailored their companies to succeed in this new reality.

✓ **Set your mission apart** – Does 2% of your profits every year to save the Amazonian Rain Forest really qualify as purpose? Perhaps, but consider the example of Revolution Foods - an ambitious company that not only provides 1.5 million meals a week to 1000 schools, but also works to teach kids about food and nutrition. To do the same, simplify your focus and make your mission something that you share more detail about – including why you believe it … and why anyone else should too.

✓ **Find the moonshots within** – Many organizations have people or teams who are already investing time and effort in their own "moonshots" but they can often fly under the radar.

Great organizations find a way to uncover those teams and individuals and then provide them with the right incentives and support to succeed ... without getting in the way. The secret is to find a way to bring those intrapreneurial innovators out of their shells and then be smart about where help is most valuable to amplify their efforts and drive results.

# Chapter 17

# OUTRAGEOUS OUTSIDERS

## *What's the Non-Obvious Trend?*

Sometimes the most innovative ideas come from outside an industry and this trend describes the rise of outsiders and their increasing willingness to say or do the things we might describe as outrageous to capture attention and influence.

Having a mustache-themed party at the end of November with your best mates is exactly the sort of idea you would expect someone to have over a pint of beer in Melbourne.

For Adam Garone – this crazy idea he first had in 2003 led to more than a successful party that year. It also induced plenty of curious stares and entertaining comments on the new mustache he had committed to grow. The attention was so pronounced, when November came around the following year he wondered: "How do we make that more meaningful?"

That question led him to seek out a charitable cause to support as part of the "Movember" party – as they had come to call the event. He found a willing participant in the Prostate Cancer Foundation of Australia, and it became an annual tradition. Year after year the tradition grew and in 2007 he brought the idea to the US – and it went viral.

The latest figures from 2016 indicate that the Movember Foundation, as it is now called, has raised over $700 million dollars for men's health and has funded over 1,000 men's health projects. After more than a decade, Garone has been interviewed numerous times on the success of the campaign and has been vocal about his lack of knowledge when he first started. "We knew nothing about charity and that actually helped us," he once shared. "It's almost impossible when you're inside the box to think outside of it."

Garone is an example of an *Outrageous Outsider* – someone who brings new ideas and actions mainly because of his or her unfiltered view of a particular topic and we are seeing these types of outsiders emerge in just about every industry.

## The Curiously Mainstream Outsider

Outsiders have been responsible for some of the biggest leaps in business and science over the past hundred years.

Albert Einstein was a patent clerk outside the closed academic circles of Physicists when he published his Special Theory of Relativity. Richard Branson was outside the airline industry when he launched Virgin Atlantic. James Dyson was an outsider to the cleaning industry when he invented his bag-less vacuum cleaner which transformed that industry.

The difference today comes from the way in which these outsiders are brought into the mainstream. Through the rise of fringe politics across the globe, outsiders are promoting minority viewpoints with authority. In the world of entrepreneurship, in many cases youth is being revered and celebrated far more than experience. Emerging research on "Generation Z" – the upcoming generation due to soon replace Millennials as our youngest workers and cultural influencers – indicates that they are heavily influenced by their love of quirkiness. (See Chapter 5 for more on this).

Welcome to the new world of the *Outrageous Outsider*, where being different and willing to say or do the things that others don't (or won't) might be the ultimate competitive advantage.

Several years ago I wrote about a trend that described the steady shift in media toward a sort of *Curated Sensationalism*. The idea was that media was becoming so sensationalized that if every story wasn't "shocking" or likely to "change your life" then it would be far less likely to receive traffic.

Today a similar effect is taking shape across politics, business and entrepreneurship when it comes to the need to be somehow outrageous. Sometimes, this need can be a good thing as it brings attention to true innovators and visionary thinkers who might otherwise have toiled in obscurity. On the other side, it is also leading to elected leaders with questionable morals, "unicorn" valuations for tech companies are that destined to fail and a bias toward focusing on the outrageous at the expense of the outsider.

To illustrate, let's consider the most problematic of the *Outrageous Outsiders* – the ones emerging in global politics.

## Outrageous Politicians

It is a great time to be an outsider if you happen to be running for office.

Across the world people are taking their frustration over establishment politics and using it to create surprising political victories, stunning cultural statements and unexpected movements. One of the most surprising of the past year was the 2016 "Brexit" vote which led the UK to declare its intention of leaving the European Union.

The move created significant cultural tension within the UK (and plenty of speculations about the financial markets in the region), but it was hardly the only big move towards outsiders in Europe. Across the continent, news stories have focused on the rise of previously fringe political groups and their new successes in moving Europe towards the far right.

In Switzerland the far-right Swiss People's Party won almost a third of votes in the national elections in 2015. The far-right party in Austria, whose motto is "Austria first," holds 40 of the 183 seats in the National Council. Poland's right-wing Law and Justice party won 39 percent of the national vote in the 2015 parliamentary elections to take power.

This shift in Europe prompted *Newsweek* magazine to host a podcast and panel discussion at the annual Wilderness Festival in Oxfordshire, England titled "Is Outsider Politics Here To Stay?" Just a month earlier, a concerned *New York Times* headline asked "How Far Is Europe Swinging To The Right?"

The question has relevance beyond Europe as well.

In the Philippines the ruthless former Mayor of Davao City Rodrigo Duterte won the Presidency on a platform that played heavily on his perceived reputation as an outsider who would shake up the country's politics.

Despite numerous public gaffes including insulting the Pope, and making insensitive comments about women and rape, he won office in a race many across the world were watching with interest. His unrefined style raised many comparisons in the media to another *Outrageous Outsider* running for office at the time in the United States: Donald Trump.

Trump is perhaps the ultimate example of a political outsider – someone who has actively disparaged politicians inside his own country, including many from his own party. Trump is a self-described "successful businessman" and has spoken on the campaign trail about everything from building a wall between the US and Mexico to making fun of women, minorities and even captured war veterans.

While he is not "Presidential" in the traditional sense of the word – his broadest appeal seems to be that he is unquestionably an outsider and not part of the same political machine that has run the federal government for the past several decades.

In an attempt to understand the widespread appeal of outsiders in politics, reporter Jeb Lund offered this insightful explanation in *The Guardian* which was originally written to apply to the UK but is equally relevant for other politicians:

> *This desire for outsiders to run our country is born of a very old, very familiar impatience with the people who are currently running it. It used to be that a politician was someone who ran for office; now that politics has made the word an epithet, everyone is running for office, but no one is a politician. They'll be whatever you want them to be, as long as you elect them to office.*

When politics is the enemy, the most outrageous of the outsiders has a chance to win … whether they possess the intellect, demeanor or experience to govern effectively or not. Brands can apply some of the same thinking of politicians to their own media campaigns and advertising.

## Kidpreneurs

If we were to study only politics, it might seem like the trend of the *Outrageous Outsider* is entirely negative, creating a world where dubiously qualified people win power for themselves and wield it in sometimes scary ways. The good news is – this trend goes far outside of politics and many of the other places where you see this embrace of outsiders end up with entirely different results.

The best example of *this* upside is considering how children are increasingly being consulted, encouraged and celebrated in business and entrepreneurship. In one prominent example, the wildly popular reality series *Shark Tank* routinely features "kidpreneurs" on the program. Kids are also encouraged at a growing range of entrepreneurship competitions and programs sponsored by schools, large brands like Google, and a recent competition sponsored and judged by billionaire Warren Buffett.

When it comes to creating new business ideas or thinking about old problems with a fresh mind, children offer an intrinsic outsider's perspective – often developing solutions unfiltered by the biases that come from experience and adulthood. This perspective is increasingly valued by companies even if these children don't start their own business, but instead provide advice for an existing one.

## Board of Kidvisors

Target is one example of a retailer that has aggressively turned to kids as advisors in remaking their business strategy around selling kids clothes. Just a few years ago the category defining brand consumers had once dubbed "Tar-zhay" for its focus on providing chic designer goods at discount prices was losing its competitive edge. In 2013 an ill-advised expansion into Canada and an attack from hackers that compromised the information of an estimated 70 million customers drove Target to a horrible holiday sales season and its worst corporate performance in over a decade.

The following year, the brand brought in new CEO Brian Cornell to reinvigorate the brand. He immediately decided to take a loss and close the operation in Canada – and soon after gave the greenlight to several bold initiatives internally, including replacing the already successful children's clothing business currently sold under the brand names Cherokee and Circo with a new brand that would be called Cat & Jack. It was a bold decision, but one that the team launching the new brand decided to tackle in an unexpected way.

Rather than simply asking kids in a focus group what they wanted or seeking design ideas by shopping in competitor's stores – the team decided to go deeper. Kids were not only invited in to help create the brand, they were also involved in the marketing campaign, sometimes even being allowed to write and direct ads online and in social media.

One of the most interesting examples is this idea of involving children who have traditionally been "outsiders" to the process of developing products made for them may seem unusual – but it is one that more and more companies are using, including one iconic brand who recently engaged kids to research and test what would eventually become their most controversial product launch ever.

## Why Girls Play Differently Than Boys

When LEGO started researching how boys and girls play, they uncovered some unpopular results. In a world that likes to talk about "gender fluidity" and how boys and girls should be treated the same, when you actually watch boys and girls play it turns out that their preferences are predictably different.

For example, when both boys and girls were asked to build a castle – most boys raced through building in order to use the figures, horses and catapults to have a battle. The girls were more focused on the structure of the castle and unimpressed with what they found inside.

When asked about the findings, LEGO spokesman Michael McNally described the surprising results this way:

> *We embarked on four years of global research with 4,500 girls and their moms. Some of the things we heard were really surprising and challenging in ways that weren't really comfortable for us as a brand. [The girls] all looked around inside the castle and they said, 'Well, there's nothing inside.' … If you think about most of the Lego models that people consider to be meant for boys, there's not a whole lot going on in there. But [the girls had] this idea of, 'There's nothing inside to do.'*

The experiments led LEGO to launch their LEGO Friends line targeted at girls. Unfortunately the move was almost immediately criticized by the media and critics – "Why Do Girls Need Special Legos?" one piece on NPR asked. The question seems like a logical one, until you look at the actual consumer response.

LEGO Friends has been a huge hit. Thanks to the new line, analysts estimate LEGO now sells many multiples more LEGOs to girls than it did about ten years ago when the number hovered at a disappointing 10% of all sales. (LEGO has not provided exact sales data publicly)

The brand bet big on the ability of kids to think like outsiders and introduce unexpected ideas. Then they maintained enough trust in this process to *follow* the advice of the outsiders.

## Hip-Hop Musicals

On Broadway in New York, the vast majority of musical shows are formulaic classics – Cats, Phantom of the Opera, The Lion King, Aladdin, Blue Man Group and others. The shows have been around for years and are what people expect. Even the new shows follow the same formula – big theatrical scenes with singing and dancing.

Then there is Hamilton.

The "hip-hop musical" inspired by a book about the life of American founding father Alexander Hamilton premiered in 2015 and has since set all kinds of records. The show has sold over $1 billion in tickets, earned creator Lin-Manuel Miranda a Pulitzer and 11 Tonys and had the most successful Broadway opening in history. As a result of the popularity, the show will be on tour throughout 2017 and 2018 to sold out audiences.

The show, which is performed entirely in rap brought hip-hop music into the mainstream for a rare moment and established Miranda as a creative force in the world of musical theater. The story of Alexander Hamilton, an outsider in his own time who emigrated from the Caribbean island of St. Croix to make his fortune in America, mirrors that of Miranda who left his native Puerto Rico to attend a New York school for the gifted and talented.

In both cases the outsider stories resonate with audiences. There is something mesmerizing about seeing a stranger out of his or her depth come into a foreign world to shine a spotlight on the things that we never thought to notice before and make transformative contributions to their countries or organizations.

Sometimes those outsiders also give us the chance to be inspired by people who seem nothing like us … until we look a bit more deeply.

## Extreme Inclusiveness

If you have ever heard people with disabilities described as "differently abled," it might seem like an exercise in political correctness run wild. Whether you like the term of not, it symbolizes the shift toward inclusiveness where those previously cast as outsiders are not only increasingly accepted, but sometimes even celebrated for their differences and their ability to lead us toward more understanding of one another.

Winnie Harlow is a powerful example.

She is a former America's Next Top Model contestant who has starred in campaigns for Desigual and Diesel while also becoming the face of a skin condition called vitiligio which causes white patches to appear on the skin. Rather than be defined by her disease, she is a role model for young girls. Last year she told an audience at the Dove Self Esteem Summit, "I don't actually think I'm ugly - I think I'm beautiful … now I've learnt to just listen to myself."

This message of self-esteem and being comfortable in your own skin is one commonly used today by other brands as well.

Haircare brand Beauty & Pin-Ups recently featured former Special Olympics athlete Katie Mead as its new face. She happens to have Down Syndrome.

Starbucks worked with the Society of Interpreters for the Deaf (SID) in Malaysia to hire 10 deaf baristas in the Bangsar district to help "create a culture of empowerment and to bring new perspectives to the workplace, which ultimately makes us a better company."

Designer handbag company Ethel + Frank launched their latest brand campaign by featuring models over 80 years old with the unexpected tagline "We Think Old Is Pretty Rad." Sesame Street this past year added a character named Julia who has autism to help educate children and adults about dealing with autistic kids.

Each of these campaigns and initiatives brings outsiders in to shift traditional assumptions and illustrate that we can appreciate one another as we are – even if age, genetics, weight or disability come between us.

## Why It Matters:

In the past, being an outsider has always offered an uneasy compromise between being a badge of honor and a recipe for loneliness. Outsiders, by definition were beyond the norm and often outcast from normal social situations. Today, outsiders are embraced for their differences. The more outrageous the better. Sometimes this leads us to idolize people who are unworthy of the attention – which is clearly on display when it comes to global politics. The more hopeful side of this trend, though, is that different viewpoints are being embraced in a way that they have traditionally not been before. Kids are respected as entrepreneurs and advisors. A Hip Hop artist can be celebrated for his artistic talent on Broadway. And brands will turn to models with skin conditions or genetic diseases because of their inner rather than outer beauty. Welcome to the world of the *Outrageous Outsider*, where we look up to and even revere those who are bold enough to look at the world differently. The more we celebrate them and their differences, the more we can create a culture that gets

ECONOMICS & ENTREPRENEURSHIP

beyond simply tolerating those different from us and helps us see the significant beauty in the differences.

## How To Use This Trend:

✓ **Consider the outsider perspective** - Outsiders, because they force us to question our long-held beliefs, are easy to dismiss. Even the loud ones may not break through if your guard is up all the time. Instead, consider reading media you disagree with or engaging in conversations with someone who believes something you don't. These are the ways to truly bring outside thinking into an organization.

✓ **Be strategically outrageous** - While this trend clearly has a downside, the skill of being "strategically outrageous" can actually help you to earn attention for your organizations best ideas and make a statement when you need to. With this trend, it is easy to focus on the "Outsider" part but the greater everyday element of it might come more from your ability to be outrageous as a brand.

✓ **Invite outsiders in** - When bringing a team together for an offsite, we often invite outsiders from disparate industries to add new ways to thinking to current processes. The tactic of getting inspiration from those outside your company or industry is one that you can use in many situations to help inspire new ideas or innovation.

# Chapter 18

# MAINSTREAM MINDFULNESS
## (ORIGINALLY CURATED 2014)

---

## *What's the Non-Obvious Trend?*

Meditation, yoga and quiet contemplation overcome their incense-
burning reputations to become powerful tools for individuals,
and companies to improve performance, wellness and motivation.

Just over two years ago, I wrote about a conference called Wisdom 2.0 that was rapidly becoming a central gathering place for evolved business leaders who were aiming to bring more mindfulness and intention to their workforces. It was about a month before the event, and I had my ticket in hand ready to participate and lead a dinner discussion, but was forced because of the timing to write about it before seeing it for myself.

I went that year, and among the many people I met and insights I gathered – the thing that struck me most during my flight home was just how much mindfulness had become more than a pet project or belief for a small group of enlightened execs. Instead, it was already a full blown industry with gurus for hire, corporate training and a growing range of apps to enable mindfulness on the go, and plenty of entrepreneurs start-ing coaching businesses or mentorship practices.

Since I first introduced this trend in 2014, the ecosystem of what we call mindfulness has continued to grow and broaden to include much more than just the practice of meditation to help clear the mind. Even in our consulting business, the demand for this type of leadership training has skyrocketed and expanded beyond simple meditation at lunch hours to a more fundamental cultural transformation to include compassionate workplaces, the power of diverse thinking, leading from the heart, and non-obvious innovation to drive employee engagement, creativity, better customer experiences and workforce harmony.

*Mainstream Mindfulness* now consumes our understanding of every-thing from what we eat to how we sleep. The trend has grown far beyond its origins and that growth inspired me to bring it back as part of this 2017 report.

As you will see in this chapter, people are going far beyond medita-tion as a means to finding some tranquility at home, work, and vacation – starting with the one thing we all do every day: sleep.

## The Sleep Revolution

A few years back the biggest cliché an executive leader would usually offer when asked to deliver career advice was usually related to working hard or believing in your dreams. "You can sleep when you're dead," was the most frequently overused phrase to capture this idea. Over the past year, the most popular new success mantra is no longer all about hustle and putting in the hours.

It is about doing the one thing all of us do but almost none of us do enough: sleep.

Business visionaries including Jeff Bezos, Warren Buffett, Bill Gates and Sheryl Sandberg have all spoken out recently about the virtues of getting enough sleep. Media mogul Ariana Huffington went one step fur-ther and wrote an entire book about the importance of sleep after having a personal experience where she was undersleeping, overworking and eventually collapsed from exhaustion.

Her experience was a wakeup call – and inspired her to write her book titled *The Sleep Revolution* where she cheekily encourages executives to "sleep your way to the top" (advocating actually sleeping and not having sex, of course).

While the book may have its critics – it is a symbol of the growing understanding that sleeping longer is not an inconvenient necessity. It may also be a strategy for success in everything from corporate health to employee engagement to weight loss. Given the deep attention on sleep, the industry of sleep is evolving and growing as well.

A report from industry research firm IBISWorld predicts that sleep labs will be a $10 billion industry by 2020. Another research report projects that sales of sleep-aid products will top $76 billion worldwide in 2019 and mattresses specifically generate more than $14 billion in the U.S. alone.

When it comes to mattresses, a range of new companies are trying to democratize and streamline the process of manufacturing and delivering mattresses altogether. Casper, Tuft & Needle, Purple, Saatva, Leesa, and YogaBed are just a handful of the most popular of the direct to consumer coil-free mattress makers. Each features a founder's story of dissatisfaction with the existing market, contempt for the typically exorbitant markups most mattress stores charge and the desire to create a better locally produced product. (Note, see Chapter 17 for the related trend of *Outrageous Outsiders* for more content on this).

Whether it is mattresses, advice books or luxury sleepwear – there is a revolution in sleep and it is driven by the growing understanding of the role that a full night's sleep has on performance, mindfulness and the broader topic of wellness itself.

## Meditative Art

One of the most surprising elements of the *Mainstream Mindfulness* trend has been the explosive growth of adult coloring books. The activity that many have started calling "Meditative Coloring" is a somewhat ceremonious way of describing the sense of calm that many people feel when taking a break from the daily stress of their lives (and their devices) simply to take time to color.

In 2017, this desire to use the creation of something as a form of meditation and relaxation is likely to spread beyond just coloring books. There are franchise bars where you can go to paint a picture over a glass of wine, and other meditative past times include knitting, scrapbooking and several other activities. No matter which of these starts to gain attention in 2017 – the point is art and creation in multiple forms can be a perfect way to relax and clear the mind and more consumers are likely to discover that.

## Building Corporate Wellness From The Inside Out

The idea of "corporate wellness" at some point several years ago might have seemed like a laughable oxymoron.

Wellness was often thought about as an antidote for the overworked. Then tech firms came along with flexible work schedules and in house masseuses and the vision for what work should be started to change. The corporation is no longer a place where tranquility goes to die. Consider this example of an office of the future...

In July of 2016, Australian property and infrastructure firm Lendlease moved into their new global headquarters in the Sydney suburb of Barangaroo. Their building was one of the first in the world to be certified under the International WELL Building Institute's Core and Shell health and wellness standard. The ambitious standard is the latest effort from the building industry to encourage the development of buildings which place people's health and wellness at the center of design.

The corporations inside those buildings are poised to spend more every year on programs to improve and optimize the health of employees as well. The umbrella idea of "Corporate Wellness" as an industry has exploded – recently being named by Inc. magazine as the #1 industry to start a business in 2016. According to a report by Rand Corporation, each dollar business owners invest in corporate wellness overall is expected to return $3.80 in savings, productivity improvements, and other benefits.

This rise in the prominence of Corporate Wellness as a category is doing more than improving the happiness of workers. It is also helping to spawn an entire industry which is attracting entrepreneurs and visionaries. Unfortunately not all of them are as "visionary" as they pretend to be.

## Spiritual Entrepreneurship

A new field of "Spiritual Entrepreneurship" is emerging where gurus, yogis, therapists, instructors and charlatans are all building businesses inspired by the principles of spirituality and mindfulness.

A quick scan of the Internet yields hundreds of personal branding websites for people who are running some sort of mindfulness coaching service or workshop. Many of them are business coaches who added a mindfulness element to what they do. Others come from a background of therapy, or physical fitness or yoga instruction. A small percentage seem to have little to no experience or training at all. Only a few provide a rigorous combination of business relevance, mindfulness expertise and the ability to train or coach transformations.

With this type of "gold rush" paced expansion, the challenge is always how to tell the trustworthy from the opportunists — and to make sure those opportunists don't drag the entire industry down. Thankfully, there are plenty of examples of people with powerful stories lending credibility to the space with their path to doing what they do.

One example is Pauline Nguyen, a Vietnamese restaurant founder and former refugee to Australia. She speaks around the world about her personal journey towards co-founding Red Lantern, the "world's most awarded Vietnamese restaurant" based in Sydney, Australia and will soon publish a book called *Grace Under Fire: The Way of the Spiritual Entrepreneur*.

She is just one of a growing number of people who are promoting the idea that the key to being a successful entrepreneur is your ability to add more spirituality and intentionality to your business. (This is related also to the idea of *Moonshot Entrepreneurship* explored in Chapter 16).

In some cases, the encouragement towards building a more spiritual company comes from an organization rather than an individual. A good example of this is the Presencing Institute, which grew out of the MIT Center for Organizational Learning. It was founded by author Peter Senge and aims to "develop and disseminate tools that help change

ECONOMICS & ENTREPRENEURSHIP

makers to create deep innovation and change."

One of the earliest projects from the group was the creation of a Global Wellbeing and Gross National Happiness (GNH) Lab, co-founded with Germany's Ministry for Economic Development and Cooperation and Bhutan's GNH Center. The Lab brings together leading innovators from developing countries, emerging economies, and industrial nations to prototype new ways of measuring and implementing well-being and progress in societies around the world.

## Focusing On Happiness

The real power of this trend comes from the intersection of mindfulness thinking in business and culture when applied proactively to the way your organization thinks. Numerous studies have demonstrated that when people are happy, they experience less pain, disease, depression, have higher income, better relationships and higher productivity. One element of this focus is the idea of happiness, and the quest to try and quantify it in more meaningful ways. Bhutan has used its metric of "Gross National Happiness," for years to measure the impact of policies on the overall well-being and happiness of its citizens and there are more countries starting to follow Bhutan's lead.

One example is Sheikh Mohammed bin Rashid Al Maktoum, ruler of the small emirate of Dubai, who created a "Happiness Index," two years ago using the installation of 23 smart devices in public buildings across the emirate as a way for residents to indicate their level of satisfaction with government services. Going one step further, last year he named the UAE's first "Minister of State For Happiness" and proclaimed that "all government policies, programmes and services must help and instill happiness and positivity in society."

In recent years, this is a metric more worldwide governments have been watching – thanks in large part to a growing cadre of research on the topic. Harvard, Mayo Clinic, and Oxford have all spent significant resources and research time focusing on the study of happiness and mindfulness and how to cultivate it. The World Happiness Report is a survey of global happiness that was first published in 2012. Now in its fifth year, the results of the survey gain worldwide attention when they are published every March in advance of UN World Happiness Day.

The report is authored by a network of leading experts in a variety of fields – economics, psychology, survey analysis, national statistics, health, public policy and more – and relies heavily on survey responses from approximately 2000 to 3000 respondents per countries analyzed. The stated aim of the report is to "review the state of happiness in the world today [and] … reflect a new worldwide demand for more attention to happiness as a criteria for government policy."

In 2016, coming out on top of the 156 countries ranked was Denmark, followed closely by Switzerland, Iceland, and Norway. The US was #13. The results of the survey, predictably, appeared in global media and were seen by millions of people.

Thanks partially to the efforts of Dubai (just one of a federation of seven emirates), the United Arab Emirates were one of only two Middle Eastern nations (along with Israel) to appear in the top 30 in the World Happiness Report at number 28. More importantly, the publication of the survey each year brings more worldwide attention to the topics of happiness and mindfulness on an international level.

## Why It Matters:

As mindfulness continues to go mainstream, this idea that the workplace, countries and even cultures can be fundamentally transformed will continue to explode. The shift is already starting to affect almost every industry, from financial services to manufacturing to professional sports, and many more. A perfect example is the unexpected move from health insurer Aetna to name Andy Lee its first Chief Mindfulness Officer - a testament to the vision of Aetna CEO Mark T. Bertolini. Examples like this one are causing a reassessment of what really matters and new industry best practices in human resources management, leadership, mentoring and business coaching. Other industries like those selling mattresses or hobby items that relate peripherally to mindfulness and wellness are also starting to see boosts simply from the association. Across 2017, the biggest impact of this trend is likely to be how many people in unexpected

ECONOMICS & ENTREPRENEURSHIP

industries start to find one another and align around the idea that focusing on mindful thinking and wellness is a non-obvious opportunity that companies can't afford to ignore.

## How to Use This Trend

✓ **Measure mindfulness beyond wellness**– It is tempting to see *Mainstream Mindfulness* as a trend purely focused on employee wellness, yet more and more of the smartest organizations are finding new ways to connect the idea of mindfulness to other business imperatives such as innovation, transformative leadership and breakthrough customer experience design. Engaging a workforce in more mindfulness can add a clarity and focus that often improves what they already do.

✓ **Make mindfulness an urgent priority**– While leading organizations such as Google, Whole Foods and LinkedIn receive a lot of credit for their mindfulness initiatives, there are plenty of others doing the same thing such as General Mills, Goldman Sachs, Intel, Medtronic, Target, SalesForce and Aetna. Ohio Congressman Tim Ryan has led a similar effort in schools in his district. No matter your industry, range of notable examples can provide the ammunition to convince reluctant leadership to commit to making mindfulness more of a priority.

✓ **Seek and create mindful moments for bonding**– Everyone wants to be part of a great company culture, but creating one is notoriously difficult. The most effective method is often offering teammates a chance to bond over something other than direct work content. Mindful workshops, offsites, attending local or national Conferences (like Wisdom 2.0) or live events can all be great ways to help put this trend to work in your organization.

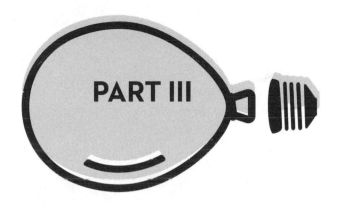

PART III

# THE TREND ACTION GUIDE

19

# INTERSECTION THINKING:
# How to Apply Trends to Your Business

"DISCOVERY CONSISTS OF SEEING WHAT EVERYBODY HAS
SEEN AND THINKING WHAT NOBODY HAS THOUGHT"

—ALBERT SZENT-GYÖRGYI, Nobel Prize–winning physician

In 2009 Tom Maas, a former marketing executive for distiller Jim Beam, finally created his perfect drink. For years he had been working on developing and promoting a new cream liquor based on the popular traditional milky cinnamon and almond drink from Latin America known as *horchata*.

This new drink, RumChata (a mashup of its primary liquor and the drink that inspired its flavors), was a mixture of light rum, dairy cream and spices like cinnamon and vanilla.

It was not an instant hit.

The drink took some inventive selling, and it was only (curiously) when bartenders started comparing its taste to the milk at the bottom of a bowl of Cinnamon Toast Crunch cereal that gained a little momentum.

Bartenders started using the liquor to create more inspired blends, which led to more liquor distributors and retailers ordering it. Meanwhile the brand ran inventive promotions like "cereal shooter bowls" designed for bars to serve RumChata based drinks and to further build the brand.

Eventually the creativity finally started working.

In 2014 a *Business Week* article noted that the drink has taken one-fifth of the market share in the $1 billion U.S. market for cream-based liquors, and even started outselling Diageo's Baileys Irish Cream (the longstanding leader) in certain regions.

More importantly, experts described the drink as a crossover game changer, due to its popularity as a mixer *and* as an ingredient for food and baking recipes.

## How to Create a Game-Changing Product

RumChata is a perfect example of the type of success that can come from putting the power of observation together with an understanding for the intersection of consumer behavior and the open space in a market.

While Maas may not have been thinking about trend curation when he came up with his product idea, we can still find some lessons in the example.

When you look backward, there are three cultural signals that may explain some of RumChata's success:

1. A growing consumer desire for authentic products with interesting backstories
2. The rising prevalence of food entertainment programming on television inspiring more creativity in home cooking
3. The increased interest across the United States in Hispanic culture and heritage

In retrospect, these observations support the arrival of a product like RumChata. Of course, putting the dots together looking backwards is easy.

The real question is: how can you do this predictably in a way that helps you create your *own* success in the future?

## An Introduction to Intersection Thinking

Trends are big ideas describing the accelerating world around us. Unfortunately, the value of big ideas are not always easily understood when it comes to applying them to real life.

Trend forecaster Chris Sanderson from *The Future Laboratory* describes trends as "profits waiting to happen." As tempting as that sounds, achieving those profits takes more than skill at uncovering, curating and describing a trend.

---

**Trends only have value if you can learn to act on them.**

---

Is a trend telling you to abandon an existing product line? Or to pivot the focus of your business? Or to stay the course in a direction that hasn't yet paid off? These are the sorts of big questions that leaders often face and they are not easy to answer.

The good news is that learning to curate trends can help offer perspective to answer those types of questions. The rest of this section is dedicated to giving you the tools, processes and knowledge to be able to apply trends in your own business and career.

Over the past several years of helping dozens of organizations and thousands of people learn to apply trends, my approach always starts with the single simple concept of "intersection thinking."

---

**Intersection thinking is a method for creating overlap between seemingly disconnected ideas in order to generate new ideas, directions and strategies for powering your own success.**

---

In other words intersection thinking is all about connecting the dots. Most of the time, I have used a workshop model to help teams and brands apply this intersection thinking to their challenges in order to create new approaches based on trends in the marketplace. Before engaging in these workshops, it is useful to share a few basic principles behind applying intersection thinking in real life.

## PRINCIPLE #1: SEE THE SIMILARITIES INSTEAD OF THE DIFFERENCES.

My friend Paolo Nagari is an intercultural intelligence expert who teaches executives the skills they need to succeed while living overseas. Unlike many other experts, however, his model doesn't rely on teaching the "dos and don'ts" of a particular culture. His belief is that succeeding in a culture other than your own takes more than memorizing lists.

Nagari's first rule for executives is all about learning to focus on the many similarities in cultures instead of the differences. It is a valuable lesson when considering how to embrace unfamiliar ideas as well.

Though the industry behind a certain trend may seem disconnected from your own, there are always more similarities than you think. When former Coca-Cola executive Jeff Dunn became president of Bolthouse Farms in 2008, for example, he walked into a billion-dollar agricultural company that had literally reinvented the carrot industry by creating "baby carrots."

By the time Dunn took over, sales of carrots (and baby carrots) were experiencing a slump and he needed a solution, so he turned to advertising agency Crispin Porter + Bogusky (CP+B).

It wasn't the usual challenge for the agency, but they were inspired by a unique idea based on a simple consumer insight: people love snacking on junk food and hate being told to eat healthier.

As CP+B creative director Omid Farhang later said in an interview "the truth about baby carrots is they possess many of the defining characteristics of our favorite junk food. They're neon orange, they're crunchy, they're dippable, they're kind of addictive."

Using this insight, CP+B built a new campaign that enticed consumers to "Eat 'Em Like Junk Food," inspired by the marketing tactics of other consumer packaged goods companies (like Coca-Cola). Baby carrots were packaged and promoted like junk food. In campaign test markets, sales immediately went up between 10% and 12%, all thanks to a campaign built from seeing the similarities between the marketing tactics for junk food and applying those to marketing baby carrots instead.

## PRINCIPLE #2: PURPOSELY LOOK AWAY FROM YOUR GOAL.

Frans Johansson is a keen observer of people and companies. His first book, *The Medici Effect*, talked beautifully about the power of intersections between diverse industries and people as a way of generating game-changing ideas, products and organizations.

In his second book, *The Click Moment*, he focused on the related idea of serendipity in our lives and what any of us might do in order to increase the chances of having our own serendipitous meetings or interactions with others.

In this second book he also retells the well-known origin story of the inspiration behind Starbucks, inspired by a trip Howard Schultz took to Milan, where he saw the dominance of the Italian espresso coffee shops on every street corner and imagined that a similar type of establishment might work outside of Italy as well.

Schultz's insight led to a pivot for Starbucks from the supplier of high-end home brewing equipment it was at the time, to a retail coffee shop. Yet the original purpose of his trip to Milan was only to attend a trade show.

It was on a chance walk from his hotel to the convention center that he noticed and became inspired by these espresso bars. His story is a perfect illustration that sometimes it is better to explore ideas outside your main goal so you can discover even bigger ideas that may be waiting around the corner (sometimes literally!).

## PRINCIPLE 3: WANDER INTO THE UNFAMILIAR.

If you happen to be walking the streets of Bangkok around 6pm on any particular day, you will see people stop in their tracks for seemingly inexplicable reasons. Ask anyone afterwards and you will quickly learn that there are two times every day when the Thai national anthem is played (8am and 6pm) and all citizens stop what they are doing and observe a moment of silence out of respect.

Once you see this cultural practice in action, it is impossible to forget.

Travel experiences are like this—whether they happen across the world from your home, or simply during a visit to a nearby yet unfamiliar place. Wandering is a form of exploration that we often think to embrace only when traveling, but it has great value on a more daily basis.

In a world where we have a mobile map in our pocket, ready to assist us with turn-by-turn directions to anywhere, wandering must be a *choice*. It is the perfect metaphor for why intersection thinking matters, and why it can be difficult as well.

Sometimes we must choose to leave our maps behind. Workshops are moments in time that can help you do that – so let's explore further exactly how and why they can be so effective.

# Why Workshops Work

**A workshop is a gathering or meeting where an individual or a group of people focus their conversation and ideation on solving a challenge or thinking in new innovative ways.**

While it may seem hard or unnecessary to bring the right people together in a room for something like a workshop (and just plain silly if you are doing it alone), there are several reasons to consider taking a workshop-driven approach to applying trends.

1. **Focus your attention.** We are all busy and usually don't have the time to be sitting around thinking about trends all day. To ensure you can have the right focused attention, it is most valuable to block out a set period of time for a workshop, even if it happens to be short. Just the act of making sure this time is scheduled and separate from your usual daily activities can help ensure that it feels (and actually becomes) significant.

2. **Set an objective.** While you don't need a step-by-step map, it is always useful to have a purpose or desired outcome defined. As the saying goes – if you don't know where you are going, how will you know when you arrive? There are many ways to engineer the structure of what you do in a workshop. I will share several of them in later chapters to help you get started. Whichever you choose, the important thing is like any good meeting, your workshop has a purpose so participants know what you aim to accomplish and make a commit to the same shared goals.

3. **Establish accountability.** Another critical reason that workshops can be so effective is that they help bring the right people together in a single moment so they can make commitments about what to do next. Accountability, of course, is equally important even if you happen to be working alone!

Almost every one of the hundreds of workshops and seminars I have given on marketing and business trends and the future starts the same way, with a presentation of trends and the situation as it is today. Yet it is important to note that most of the time, *the ultimate goal in a workshop should not be to uncover new trends.*

A workshop is most useful after you have *already* used the process in the first part of the book to curate your own trends, or selected trends produced by others (such as those featured in Part II of this book) or trends from other reputable sources. The goal of any trend workshop should be to take those trends and determine how to put them into action to solve your business challenges.

## 5 Keys to Running a Great Trend Workshop

When using a workshop model to guide your thinking, there are a few basic ground rules to keep in mind:

1. **Always have an unbiased facilitator** – It is easy to assume that the person closest to the issue will be the right person to lead a workshop, but this is often not true. Instead, the best workshop facilitators are individuals who can lead a discussion, keep a conversation on track and ask provocative questions without being biased or intentionally leading a group toward a particular answer or point of view.

2. **Encourage sharing, not critiquing** – We have all heard the common cliché that there are "no bad ideas in a brainstorm." That's not technically true. There *are* bad ideas, off-strategy ideas, impossible ideas and useless ideas. Unfortunately, they are rarely easy to distinguish in the real time environment of most workshops. For that reason, the best mentality to encourage for all participants is one where everyone commits to sharing ideas rather than wasting time and energy trying to critique them too. Capture first, critique later.

3. **Adopt a "yes and" mindset** – Improve actors always talk about the importance of collaborating with others in a scene

by always saying "yes and" instead of "yes but" (its far more negative cousin). This additive approach allows you to build upon what others have shared instead of breaking it down, and it is one of the consistent hallmarks of great and effective workshops as well.

4. **Prepare like a pro** – If you have ever heard the phrase "garbage in, garbage out"—you should know this applies tenfold to workshops. If you have not prepared the right materials, insights and questions before a workshop, you will rarely be able to generate great value. This doesn't necessarily mean spending months on research, but you should have the right background to ask the right questions and focus the conversation on the most critical topics and always keep moving forward.

5. **Recap and summarize** – One of the worst things to do after committing the time and expense to running a workshop is to let everyone in the room leave without summarizing what took place over the time you shared together. It is the role of the facilitator to summarize the conversation, recap any action items and ensure that everyone who spent their precious time participating understands what they collectively achieved and what will need to happen next in order to keep the momentum going.

## About The Four Models of Trend Workshops

Now that we have talked about what it takes to run a great workshop, let's focus on the types of workshops most commonly used to help apply trends to organizations.

- **Customer Journey Mapping Trend Workshop** – Building a step-by-step understanding of how your customers interact with you so you can apply trends to each step of the process.
- **Brand Storytelling Trend Workshop** – Developing a powerful brand story or message designed to resonate with

customers based on understanding and using current trends.

- **Business Strategy Trend Workshop** – Creating a new go-to-market or product-launch strategy or making changes to a business model or revenue model informed by current trends and new competitive situations.
- **Company Culture Trend Workshop** – Planning your career or optimizing and improving an internal company culture and team based on current trends.

In the original 2015 hardcover edition of Non-Obvious, each workshop was outlined in detail through four additional chapters. For the sake of brevity those chapters are not included in this edition. However, if you would still like to read them you can visit www.nonobviousbook.com/resources to download each of these chapters together in a single free bonus PDF.

## Note For Small Teams

Although most of this chapter and the bonus PDF are specifically written from the point of view of having multiple participants in each type of workshop, many of the lessons in these chapters can be easily applied to small businesses individually as well.

It may be tempting to dismiss the value of workshops or even intersection thinking if you happen to be on your own or part of a tiny team, but I encourage you to give these approaches a chance anyway. Just because you don't have a large group of team members doesn't mean you can't use the benefits of intersection thinking and workshops to power your business. There is never a bad time to break from your normal routine and dedicate time through a workshop to strategizing for the future.

# THE 7 BEST TREND RESOURCES
# YOU NEED TO BOOKMARK

Despite the skepticism with which I often approach trend reports from so-called gurus, there are handful of amazingly valuable sources for trend forecasting and techniques that I have drawn upon heavily over the years. Some have already been cited elsewhere in this book, however in the interests of simplicity, I am including a full list of some of my favorite resources below. (*Note:* Several top sources such as Iconoculture, Future Hunters, or Springwise have been omitted from this list because most of their research is accessible only to subscribers and not the general public.)

The following organizations and individuals publish consistently insightful ideas and forecasts worth paying attention to. Each is on my must-read list every year and never fails to offer several ideas that inform my thinking annually as I prepare the *Non-Obvious Trend Report.*

### 1. Trendwatching.com (trendwatching.com)
This is hands-down the most useful trend and forecasting resource online. Through a network of thousands of spotters all over the world, this is the one resource that I consistently find insightful, valuable and extremely well researched. Visit their site and subscribe to receive their excellent free monthly reports. If you work for an organization that can afford it, pay to access their premium service and use it.

2. **PSFK (www.psfk.com)**

Ever since I first met founder Piers Fawkes at an event more than a decade ago, I have been impressed with the thinking that he and his team compile on big topics like the future of retail and the future of work. Several of their reports are published in partnership with sponsors, which means they are freely available, but even just browsing their usually excellent blog will inspire you with new ideas, curated observations and plenty of stories worth saving for later aggregation.

3. *Megatrends* **by John Naisbitt**

There is a reason why this book about trends and the future has been a bestseller for the past three decades. In the book, Naisbitt paints a fascinating future portrait of the world as he saw it back in the early '80s. Despite the many years that have passed since the book was first published, it remains a valuable read both for the prescience of his ideas and how he manages to capture the spirit of his time while also producing a startling accurate vision of the future.

4. *The Trend Forecaster's Handbook* **by Martin Raymond**

There isn't really a textbook for trend forecasting, but if there were, this full-color large-format volume from Martin Raymond would come pretty close. It has a hefty price tag (like most textbooks), but the content is beautifully organized and it comes closest to presenting a dictionary-style compilation of everything you can imagine needing to know about trend forecasting. From interviews with top futurists to highly useful sidebars (like how to select and interview an expert panel), this book shares so much insight that it's one of those books which belongs on your bookshelf.

5. **Cool Hunting (www.coolhunting.com)**

If you have ever been to one of those beautifully authentic farmer's markets where the produce is amazingly fresh, but the organization is a bit haphazard and confusing – then you'll appreciate the good and bad of Cool Hunting. The site has amazing content and is guaranteed to spark new ideas for you anytime you visit, but you'll have to navigate the busy design and minimal organization alongside those sparks of brilliance. If you can find the patience to browse the site instead of searching, though, you will find the content to be completely inspirational.

### 6. The Cool Hunter (www.thecoolhunter.co.uk)

Despite its name, this site has no affiliation with Cool Hunting. Aside from sharing a compendium of ideas, the structure of the sites couldn't be more different. On The Cool Hunter, all the blog posts are cleanly presented in very specific categories from "Exotic Places" to "Architecture." Each post is highly visual and it is easy to browse from story to story. As a result, the experience of navigating the site is a bit like going to a perfectly organized library and pulling random ideas off the shelf.

### 7. SlideShare (www.slideshare.com)

Almost every flawed, lazy or overly ambitious trend report I have ever read was one I found on Slideshare.com, so it probably seems like an odd choice to add to my list of must-read resources, but the fact is you can get a lot of great insights on SlideShare. Some of them relate to trend predictions that are of little value, but learning to *see through* them is a valuable skill in itself. Outside of that, there are plenty of deep, insightful presentations that can offer ideas about new industries and markets, or take you inside an unfamiliar subject in a visual and easy-to-read way.

For an online list of all the sources included here (as well as several new sources added since this list was published), please visit:

WWW..NONOBVIOUSBOOK.COM/RESOURCES

# ANTI-TRENDS:
# The Flip Side Of Trends

"THERE ARE TRIVIAL TRUTHS AND THERE ARE GREAT TRUTHS.
THE OPPOSITE OF A TRIVIAL TRUTH IS PLAINLY FALSE. THE
OPPOSITE OF A GREAT TRUTH IS ALSO TRUE."

—NEILS BOHR, Nobel Prize–winning physicist

From the end of September until the beginning of November, the Piedmont region of Italy is one of the most popular foodie destinations in the world for two reasons. The first is the famous Barolo wines produced from the native Nebbiolo grape and the second comes in October, when the town of Alba hosts its annual White Truffle Fair.

Truffles are a favorite decadent ingredient for top chefs and white truffles are the rarest—sometimes costing as much as $2000 per pound. Truffles from Alba are alternately described by chefs as "sublime" and "unlike anything else in the world." The Barolo wines too are considered Italy's best, called the "king of wines" for centuries.

Yet as amazing as these two Piedmont region delicacies are, there is one critical problem the region can't control: they are never both at their relative prime at the same time – because they require opposite kinds of weather.

Truffles are best after a wet summer, while wine is best after a dry and hot summer. As a result, any summer cannot be equally good for both wine *and* truffles.

## Flip Thinking and Anti-Trends

In this book, I have shared a process for uncovering trends that affect the world around us, and advice on how to use them to power your business and career. Perhaps while reading one of these trends, you thought of an example that seemed to do the exact opposite of what the trend was describing. Or that the impact of one trend made another less valuable – like the truffles and wine.

Just like Piedmont's delicacies, there is often an opposing force that balances out trends, and it comes from people and companies that see what everyone else is doing and choose to do the opposite. Sometimes we hear it called "flip thinking," a term used most popularly by author Dan Pink. In one instance, he used it to describe a teacher who "flipped" the classroom by assigning math lectures via YouTube video as homework and actually *doing* the problems together in class.

Flip thinking will always be present, and for every trend someone will usually find an example of the exact opposite. This is not a flaw in trend prediction but it would be natural to wonder: if we have invested all this work into curating and describing trends, how can we be sure they matter when it seems so easy to find examples of the opposite?

## Breaking Trends

Trends are not like mathematical theories. They are describing a behaviour or occurence that is accelerating and will matter more and more, but they are not hard and fast rules of culture or behavior. There will always be outliers.

The point of curating trends is to see what others don't, to predict a future that can inspire new thinking. There is an interesting opportunity, though, that arises from being able to use this truth of "flip thinking" for yourself.

**Understanding trends not only empowers you to use them positively, but also to intentionally break them and do the opposite when it's an appropriate way to stand out.**

Pablo Picasso famously declared that each of us should aim to "learn the rules like a pro so you can break them like an artist."

The clown in an ice-skating show, for example, often needs to be the most talented in order to execute fake jumps and falls while still remaining under control. Similarly, your ability to know the trends may give you the insight you need to bend or break them strategically.

This is, after all, a book about thinking in new and different ways. Taking a trend and aiming to embrace its opposite certainly qualifies.

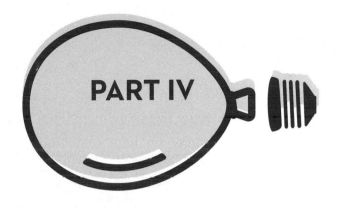

# PREVIOUS TREND REPORT SUMMARIES 2011-2016

# OVERVIEW:
## How to Read These Past Trend Reports

⋅——⋅

"THE EVENTS OF THE PAST CAN BE MADE TO PROVE
ANYTHING IF THEY ARE ARRANGED IN A SUITABLE PATTERN."
—A. J. P. Taylor, Historian

There was a moment several years ago when I was on stage after having just presented a talk about trends and how to predict the future when a gentleman stood up to ask me a question. "It must be easy," he started "to publish your trend report when you get to change them every year. How do you know whether any of them were actually right?"

His question was a fair one. After all, there is plenty of evidence to suggest the experts routinely miss predictions and are often just plain wrong. What makes my method or the past trends I have curated any different? The only truthful way to answer that is to take a look backward.

In this section, you'll see a candid review of every one of my previously predicted trends from the past six years of the *Non-Obvious Trend Report*. While some of the descriptions have been edited for space considerations, none of the intentions or meanings have been updated or revisited since the trend was first published.

Each trend is accompanied by a "Trend Longevity Rating" which aims to measure how much the trend as originally described still applies or has value in 2017. Predictably, the more recent trends fared better than the older trends – but the process of going backward and taking an honest look at past research was illuminating.

In assessing these trends, my aim was to treat them in as unbiased a way as possible. Where one did not accelerate the way I predicted, I did my best to admit that openly. It is, of course, nearly impossible to grade yourself in isolation – so I have also gathered the feedback from hundreds of professionals who have listened to me share my "Haystack Method" and the trends that resulted from it. I took notes as they participated in workshops trying to apply these trends to their own businesses, and recorded some of the probing questions about each trend.

In addition, I made it a habit when collecting ideas to also save stories and examples of trends that I had already published – so I could see just how many more relevant examples would come up since it was originally curated. This story gathering is what helped me decide which of my previous trends to revisit in this new edition.

If there is anything that has helped me get better at curating new trends year after year, it is this annual ritual of reviewing, grading and critiquing past trends.

As I shared early in this book, the beautiful thing about trends is that new trends don't replace old ones. Rather, they all present an evolving view of the world and individual "non-obvious" trends either become perfectly obvious (and commonly understood) over time, or they fail to accelerate and sometimes fade away.

Either way, the best case usage for trends is as a spark for new ideas and as an instigator for innovation.

I hope you enjoy this look backward at past years of the Non-Obvious Trend Report.

# PREVIOUSLY PREDICTED TREND SUMMARIES (2011-2016)

| 2011 NON-OBVIOUS TRENDS | 2012 NON-OBVIOUS TRENDS |
| --- | --- |
| LIKEONOMICS | CORPORATE HUMANISM |
| APPROACHABLE CELEBRITY | ETHNOMIMICRY |
| DESPERATE SIMPLIFICATION | SOCIAL LONELINESS |
| ESSENTIAL INTEGRATION | POINTILLIST FILMMAKING |
| RISE OF CURATION | MEASURING LIFE |
| VISUALIZED DATA | CO-CURATION |
| CROWDSOURCED INNOVATION | CHARITABLE ENGAGEMENT |
| INSTANT PR & CUSTOMER SERVICE | MEDICI MARKETING |
| APP-FICATION OF THE WEB | DIGITAL AFTERLIFE |
| RE-IMAGINING CHARITY | REAL-TIME LOGISTICS |
| EMPLOYEES AS HEROES | SOCIAL ARTIVISM |
| LOCATIONCASTING | CIVIC ENGAGEMENT 2.0 |
| BRUTAL TRANSPARENCY | TAGGING REALITY |
| ADDICTIVE RANDOMNESS | CHANGESOURCING |
| CULTING OF RETAIL | RETAIL THEATER |

| 2013 NON-OBVIOUS TRENDS | 2014 NON-OBVIOUS TRENDS |
| --- | --- |
| OPTIMISTIC AGING | DESPARATE DETOX |
| HUMAN BANKING | MEDIA BINGING |
| MEFUNDING | OBSESSIVE PRODUCTIVITY |
| BRANDED INSPIRATION | LOVABLE IMPERFECTION |
| BACKSTORYTELLING | BRANDED UTILITY |
| HEALTHY CONTENT | SHAREABLE HUMANITY |
| DEGREE-FREE LEARNING | CURATED SENSATIONALISM |
| PRECIOUS PRINT | DISTRIBUTED EXPERTISE |
| PARTNERSHIP PUBLISHING | ANTI-STEREOTYPING |
| MICROINNOVATION | PRIVACY PARANOIA |
| SOCIAL VISUALIZATION | OVERQUANTIFIED LIFE |
| HEROIC DESIGN | MICRODESIGN |
| HYPER-LOCAL COMMERCE | SUBSCRIPTION COMMERCE |
| POWERED BY WOMEN | INSTANT ENTREPRENEURS |
| SHOPTIMIZATION | COLLABORATIVE ECONOMY |

| 2015 NON-OBVIOUS TRENDS | 2016 NON-OBVIOUS TRENDS |
| --- | --- |
| EVERYDAY STARDOM | E-MPULSE BUYING |
| SELFIE CONFIDENCE | STRATEGIC DOWNGRADING |
| MAINSTREAM MINDFULNESS | OPTIMISTIC AGING |
| BRANDED BENEVOLENCE | B2BEYOND |
| REVERSE RETAIL | PERSONALITY MAPPING |
| RELUCTANT MARKETING | BRANDED UTILITY |
| GLANCEABLE CONTENT | MAINSTREAM MULTICULTURALISM |
| MOOD MATCHING | EARNED CONSUMPTION |
| EXPERIMEDIA | ANTI-STEREOTYPING |
| UNPERFECTION | VIRTUAL EMPATHY |
| PREDICTIVE PROTECTION | DATA OVERFLOW |
| ENGINEERED ADDICTION | HEROIC DESIGN |
| SMALL DATA | INSOURCED INCUBATION |
| DISRUPTIVE DISTRIBUTION | AUTOMATED ADULTHOOD |
| MICRO CONSUMPTION | OBSESSIVE PRODUCTIVITY |

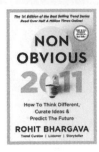

**Original Publication Date:** *January 2, 2011*
**Original Format:** *Visual Presentation Only*
**Full Book:** *www.nonobviousbook.com/2011*

## THE BACKSTORY

This first edition of the Non-Obvious Trend Report was inspired by five years of blogging. I released it exclusively in a visual presentation format and heavily featured marketing and social media trends that I had written about throughout 2010. The trends were far more limited in scope than later editions of the trend report and featured less description and less actionable advice. They were also not separated into subcategories, but instead presented as a full list of 15 marketing and social media trends that mattered. Each trend featured a short description, a few example stories and some quick tips for brands on how to use the lessons in the report to power their marketing strategy.

## RETROSPECTIVE: HOW ACCURATE WAS THIS REPORT?

The report was one of the first to predict the rise in importance of content marketing through curation and also predicted the rapid growth of real-time customer service through social media. It analyzed the increasing number of marketing campaigns featuring employees as a sign of corporate humanity, and introduced the idea of how social media was making unreachable celebrities more connected and approachable. Overall, there were relatively few big misses or trends that completely imploded or reversed themselves. The biggest idea from the report was undoubtedly the first trend *Likeonomics*, which ultimately inspired me to write a book of the same name (released in 2012) to build the idea out further.

*NOTE – There were no icons for trends in this report, and so the individual trend longevity ratings for this year are not included in this section. You can still see the full assessments by visiting the URL at the top of this page.*

# The 2012 Non-Obvious
# Trend Report Overview

**Original Publication Date:** *January 2, 2012*
**Original Format:** *Visual Presentation Only*
**Full Book:** *www.nonobviousbook.com/2012*

## THE BACKSTORY

This second year of the trend report featured a broader look at business beyond marketing and brought together the worlds of corporate marketing, charitable causes, the marketing of death and more. Like the first report, it was only released exclusively in visual presentation format online. This report tackled the sensitive yet emerging field of the digital afterlife of loved ones who have passed on, as well as the rising sense of social loneliness that people felt. In contrast to my 2011 report, the theme of this report moved a little further away from marketing campaigns and took a more human tone as many of the trends featured cultural or consumer-based trends instead of those inspired by what brand marketers were already doing.

## RETROSPECTIVE: HOW ACCURATE WAS THIS REPORT?

The 2012 report had a few big hits and several big misses. The overall trends that centered on the growth of humanity in companies and consumers worked out well. This report was one of the first to explore the potential of big data to impact everything from optimizing supply chain logistics to measuring and quantifying every aspect of our lives. On the flip side, the trends that made bigger bets on well named but overly quirky niche concepts like *Pointillist Filmmaking* or *Social Artivism* did not quantifiably catch fire, either in adoption or in the behaviors they described.

*NOTE – There were no icons for trends in this report, and so the individual trend longevity ratings for this year are not included in this section. You can still see the full assessments by visiting the URL at the top of this page.*

# The 2013 Non-Obvious Trend Report Overview

**Original Publication Date:** *December 10, 2012*
**Original Format:** *eBook + Visual Presentation*
**Full Book:** *www.nonobviousbook.com/2013*

## THE BACKSTORY

In the third year of producing the trend report, the level of detail exploded as my full report went from about 20 pages to over 100. The report featured more examples, more analysis-and 3 bonus trends – which are available online. While this edition of the Trend Report did not originally use the five categories, for alignment I retroactively applied the five categories to the trends.

The report was still delivered primarily in a visual presentation format, but this year there was an accompanying ebook available for sale on Amazon for the first time featuring not only the trends, but also suggestions on how to put them into action.

Thanks to the online audience built from the first two editions, this third edition ebook was an immediate best seller on Amazon, remaining the number-one book in the market research category for eight straight weeks after launch and was viewed more than 200,000 times online. The clean visuals, level of detail and growing reputation for the annual report also resulted in plenty of sharing and comments online.

## RETROSPECTIVE: HOW ACCURATE WAS THIS REPORT?

Developing the trends for 2013 was a more deliberate process requiring more research and a higher standard of proof before including any particular trend in the report. Topics featured in the 2013 report included the future of print publishing, the rise of women in business, authenticity in the banking sector, hyper-local commerce and the evolution of the travel industry.

# 2013 NON-OBVIOUS TRENDS OVERVIEW – SUMMARY

## WHAT IS A TREND?
*A trend is a unique curated observation about the accelerating present*

**CULTURE & CONSUMER BEHAVIOR** - Trends in how we see ourselves and patterns in popular culture

**Optimistic Aging**

**Human Banking**

**MeFunding**

**MARKETING & SOCIAL MEDIA** - Trends in how brands are trying to influence and engage consumers

**Branded Inspiration**

**Backstorytelling**

**Healthy Content**

**MEDIA & EDUCATION** - Trends in content and information impacting how we learn or are entertained

**Degree-Free Learning**

**Precious Print**

**Partnership Publishing**

**TECHNOLOGY & DESIGN** - Trends in technology innovation and product design impacting our behavior

**Microinnovation**

**Social Visualization**

**Heroic Design**

**ECONOMICS & ENTREPRENEURSHIP** - Trends in business models, startups and careers affecting the future of work or money

**Hyper-Local Commerce**

**Powered By Women**

**Shoptimization**

**OPTIMISTIC AGING**

**What's the Trend?**
A wealth of new online content and new social networks inspire people of all ages to feel more optimistic about getting older.

**Trend Longevity Rating:**
*This trend was important enough for me to select and bring back in my 2016 report – but as I shared in the rating for this trend from that year, the sense of optimism about what will be achievable in life has remained for the older population but over the past year it was tempered by increasing fears about the macro future of things like the environment, politics, the economy and security.*

**HUMAN BANKING**

**What's the Trend?**
Aiming to change years of growing distrust, banks finally uncover their human side by taking a more simple and direct approach to services and communication and develop real relationships with their customers.

**Trend Longevity Rating:**
*Every new financial crisis underscores the importance of more human interactions between us and our financial institutions. While this trend has been happening across multiple industries, the effect on banking (and consumer banks in particular) has been pronounced.*

**MEFUNDING**

**What's the Trend?**
Crowdfunding evolves beyond films or budding entrepreneurs to offer anyone the opportunity to seek financial support to do anything from taking a life-changing trip to paying for a college education.

**Trend Longevity Rating:**
*While the many sites featured as part of this trend remain available for people to use, the trend didn't quite explode in the way I predicted. This is one of those ideas that sees a steady stream of attention and usage but never quite accelerated beyond that.*

# 2013 Marketing & Social Media Trends

**BRANDED INSPIRATION**

### What's the Trend?
Brands create awe-inspiring moments, innovative ideas and dramatic stunts to capture attention and demonstrate their values to the world.

### Trend Longevity Rating:
*While 2013 was a watershed year for brands to use big moments for inspiration, the new model for this involves creating an effort for social good and standing for something bigger versus simply creating an entertaining moment of theater to inspire.*

---

**BACKSTORYTELLING**

### What's the Trend?
Organizations discover that taking people behind the scenes of their brand and history is one of the most powerful ways to inspire loyalty.

### Trend Longevity Rating:
*As social platforms splinter but also grow in popularity, the necessity for brands to share their backstory in multiple ways continues to grow. Add this to the rising consciousness of consumers about the ethical business practices of companies and desire for a reason to believe in a brand's mission and this trend is and will continue to be critical.*

---

**HEALTHY CONTENT**

### What's the Trend?
In an effort to satisfy increasingly empowered patients who have become unreachable through pure marketing or advertising, Healthcare organizations have begun create more useful and substantial health content.

### Trend Longevity Rating:
*In the healthcare industry, content continues to be golden because empowered patients gain more confidence and increasingly turn to the web before seeking information from other sources. There are no signs that this behavior will diminish in the near and farther future.*

**DEGREE-FREE LEARNING**

**What's the Trend?**
The quality of e-learning content explodes as more students consider alternatives to traditional college educations.

**Trend Longevity Rating:**
*Learning and higher education are simultaneously changed by this growth of people who choose to learn new skills and industries without requiring a degree to display at the end of it. While this has not overtaken traditional degree-granting programs, it continues to gain in popularity.*

**PRECIOUS PRINT**

**What's the Trend?**
With an ever increasing digital culture, the few interactions we have with the print medium become ever more valuable.

**Trend Longevity Rating:**
*The basic human behavior outlined in this trend—that we place even more value on the things that are printed because they are so much more rare—continues year after year ... so much so that this was one of the trends I brought back for the 2017 report with more nuances around print in various other situations.*

**PARTNERSHIP PUBLISHING**

**What's the Trend?**
Aspiring authors, lacking a platform, and seasoned publishing professionals, in need of ambitious talent and content, team up to create a new "do-it-together" model of publishing.

**Trend Longevity Rating: B+**
*This trend inspired me to start Ideapress Publishing as a new venture to bring together some of the top tier freelance publishing talent and authors. There were plenty of other similar ventures to explore this idea as well - but the focus on this as an exciting new area waned somewhat over the years since this trend was first published.*

# 2013 Technology & Design Trends

**MICROINNOVATION**

### What's the Trend?
Thinking small becomes the new competitive advantage as slight changes to features or benefits creates big value.

### Trend Longevity Rating:
*If anything, this trend has accelerated dramatically in recent years as more brands adopt a lean startup mentality that encourages them to make incremental changes to products in ways that can deliver value. The quest to do this in a meaningful way is ongoing, particularly in the technology industry.*

A-

### SOCIAL VISUALIZATION

### What's the Trend?
In an attempt to make data more accessible, new tools and technologies allow people to visualize content as part of their social profiles and online conversations.

### Trend Longevity Rating:
*Visual interfaces continue to be commonplace and popular. This is one of those trends that was emerging at the time when it was first written but today more than four years later is seems so obvious that it hardly qualifies to be called a trend – yet that remains perhaps the ultimate test of longevity for a trend, and reaching this level of ubiquity is one sign of success.*

A

**HEROIC DESIGN**

### What's the Trend?
Design takes a leading role in the introduction of new products, ideas and campaigns to help change the world.

### Trend Longevity Rating:
*The growth of design thinking as well as an increasingly reliance from the global community on seeing solutions to global problems posed by designers led me to bring this trend back for my 2016 report. Since that time, the importance of design serving a "heroic" purpose to solve society's biggest challenges has continued.*

A

**HYPER LOCAL COMMERCE**

**What's the Trend?**
New services and technology make it easier for anyone to invest in local businesses and buy from local merchants.

**Trend Longevity Rating:**
*Whether you examine this trend in relation to the growth of local commerce or as fueled by investment and interest in mobile commerce platforms and experience, the fact is consumer experiences continue to become more local more custom and more personal ... and so this trend is likely to continue.*

---

**POWERED BY WOMEN**

**What's the Trend?**
Business leaders, pop-culture, and ground-breaking new research intersect to prove that our ideal future will be led by strong and innovative women working on the front lines.

**Trend Longevity Rating:**
*There is no denying the role of women in business, culture and politics has grown year after year. Today there are more female leaders, role models and celebrated citizens than ever before—and it is a wonderful thing leading to interesting related trends, like this past year's Fierce Femininity trend.*

---

**SHOPTIMIZATION**

**What's the Trend?**
The proliferation of smart phones coupled with new mobile apps and startups let consumers optimize and enhance the process of online shopping for faster purchases of everything from fashion, to home goods to medical prescriptions.

**Trend Longevity Rating:**
*Thanks to increasing competition among retailers and a rising tide of new productivity tools online, the task of optimizing each of our shopping experiences has continued to be a top priority leading to better mobile first interfaces, one button shopping apps, and the ability to buy anything anywhere at the touch of a button.*

NON OBVIOUS 2014

How To Think Different, Curate Ideas & Predict The Future

**ROHIT BHARGAVA**
Trend Curator | Listener | Storyteller

## The 2014 Non-Obvious Trend Report Overview

**Original Publication Date:** *February 18, 2014*
**Original Format:** *eBook + Visual Presentation*
**Full Book:** *www.nonobviousbook.com/2014*

### THE BACKSTORY

This fourth edition of the Non-Obvious Trend Report was expanded to feature categories for trends for the first time instead of simply listing 15 in random order. Those categories are the ones used in every consecutive report since that year.

In an effort to build visibility, in 2014 I also made the full report freely available online with a bonus ebook available for sale on Amazon. The corresponding ebook among those who needed to implement and put the trends into action.

This edition also corresponded with an exponential growth in the volume of public speaking and workshops I was being invited to deliver and was also the year that I left Ogilvy (after 8 years) and finally started my own group to focus on trend research, keynote speaking, consulting and teaching full time.

### RETROSPECTIVE: HOW ACCURATE WAS THIS REPORT?

Due to the new category driven approach, I was able to be more disciplined with my predictions. *Desperate Detox, Subscription Commerce, Collaborative Economy, Obsessive Productivity, Branded Utility* and *Curated Sensationalism* were all big trends that described entire movements and they received a lot of attention. This report also incorporated some of the healthcare specific trend research that my co-author Fard Johnmar and I published that year in our industry vertical book about trends in health called *ePatient 2015*.

# 2014 NON-OBVIOUS TRENDS OVERVIEW – SUMMARY

## WHAT IS A TREND?
*A trend is a unique curated observation about the accelerating present*

**CULTURE & CONSUMER BEHAVIOR** - Trends in how we see ourselves and patterns in popular culture

**Desperate Detox**

**Media Binging**

**Obsessive Productivity**

**MARKETING & SOCIAL MEDIA** - Trends in how brands are trying to influence and engage consumers

**Lovable Imperfection**

**Branded Utility**

**Shareable Humanity**

**MEDIA & EDUCATION** - Trends in content and information impacting how we learn or are entertained

**Curated Sensationalism**

**Distributed Expertise**

**Anti-Stereotyping**

**TECHNOLOGY & DESIGN** - Trends in technology innovation and product design impacting our behavior

**Privacy Paranoia**

**Overquantified Life**

**Microdesign**

**ECONOMICS & ENTREPRENEURSHIP** - Trends in business models, startups and careers affecting the future of work or money

**Subscription Commerce**

**Instant Entrepreneurs**

**Collaborative Economy**

**DESPERATE DETOX**

**What's the Trend?**
Consumers try to more authentically connect with others and seek out moments of reflection by intentionally disconnecting from the technology surrounding them.

**Trend Longevity Rating:**
*Technology is only becoming more omnipresent in our lives, and this trend was so impactful that it was an easy selection as one to bring back in 2017 to include in this year's report.*

**MEDIA BINGING**

**What's the Trend?**
As more media and entertainment is available on any device on demand, consumers binge and are willing to pay extra for the convenience.

**Trend Longevity Rating:**
*Streaming options continue to expand and consumer behavior follows. Media Binging is a trend that will continue and has also influenced some later trends that have been featured in subsequent reports, such as this year's trend of Deep Diving.*

**OBSESSIVE PRODUCTIVITY**

**What's the Trend?**
With thousands of life-optimizing apps and instant advice from social media–savvy self-help gurus, becoming more productive has become the ultimate obsession.

**Trend Longevity Rating:**
*The past few years have brought plenty of new bestselling books talking about optimizing your life, hacking your daily chores and saving time. To say people continue to obsess over their own productivity is becoming an understatement – so this trend is clearly continuing to have a big impact.*

# 2014 Marketing & Social Media Trends

## LOVABLE IMPERFECTION

**What's the Trend?**
Consumers seek out true authenticity and reward minor imperfections in products, personalities and brands by showing greater loyalty and trust.

**Trend Longevity Rating:**
*While this was the first year that this trend was predicted, it was so powerful that a version of it was included in the 2015 report (Unperfection) and it is making another appearance in my latest report because of its continued importance.*

## BRANDED UTILITY

**What's the Trend?**
Brands use content marketing and greater integration between marketing and operations centers to augment promotions with real ways to add value to customer's lives.

**Trend Longevity Rating:**
*As content marketing continues to dramatically change the way that marketers communicate with their audiences, there have been dozens more examples of brands using this trend. It's impact was also important enough to bring it back to include in my 2016 Trend Report.*

## SHARABLE HUMANITY

**What's the Trend?**
Content shared on social media gets more emotional as people share amazing examples of humanity and brands inject more of it into marketing communications efforts.

**Trend Longevity Rating:**
*This was one of the trends from the previous year that was negatively affected by the fatigue some media consumers are starting to experience from overly dramatic media stories and click-baiting headlines. Though we continue to find human stories irresistible to read and share, this trend no longer has the impact it once did when first predicted.*

### What's the Trend?
As the line between news and entertainment blurs, smart curation displaces journalism as engaging content is paired with sensational headlines to drive millions of views.

### Trend Longevity Rating:
*Media continues to deliver over-the-top headlines and sensationalism that continue to negatively affect consumer trust in media – but consumer sentiment has turned against this type of technique. Despite the fact that its effectiveness is rooted in an understanding of human psychology, the growing awareness of exactly why these links are so irresistible is created a backlash effect.*

**CURATED SENSATIONALISM**

### What's the Trend?
The idea of expertise itself shifts to become more inclusive, less academic and more widely available on demand and in real time.

### Trend Longevity Rating:
*Learning through experts online in many formats is still a big trend and one that is powering some of the fastest growing learning platforms online today (including many profiled in this original trend). We officially have on demand access to experts in many ways online and it is a beautiful thing.*

**DISTRIBUTED EXPERTISE**

### What's the Trend?
Across media and entertainment, traditional gender roles are being reversed, assumptions about alternative lifestyles are being challenged, and perceptions of how people are defines evolve in new ways.

### Trend Longevity Rating:
*The reversing of gender roles continues to be a big opportunity for brands to get their messaging right, or wrong, when it comes to speaking to these diverse groups through marketing and communications – but the broader aspects of this trend were what encouraged me to bring it back in 2016 and continues to be relevant.*

**ANTI-STEREOTYPING**

**PRIVACY PARANOIA**

### What's the Trend?
New data breaches are leading to a new global sense of paranoia about what governments and brands know about us—and how they might use this big data in potentially harmful ways.

### Trend Longevity Rating:
*As more tools enter the market to help consumers protect their information and take back control of their privacy, this paranoia is shifting to empowerment. All the warnings and attention on privacy are leading some people to ignore the warnings while others take back control. Either way, "paranoia" is no longer the ideal term to describe our relationship to privacy.*

**OVERQUANTIFIED LIFE**

### What's the Trend?
As big data leads brands to overload data with cute infographics and superficial analysis, they also add more confusion about what all this data really means, and how it can inform decisions in real life.

### Trend Longevity Rating:
*Connecting all the data we collect on ourselves in a meaningful way continues to be a challenge, and we are indeed still "overquantified" but there are new ways that this data is being put to use and reflected back as a useful mirror of our activities. The more these things happen, the less "overquantified" we feel as consumers.*

**MICRODESIGN**

### What's the Trend?
As communication becomes more visual, design gains more respect and becomes an everyday business requirement. At the same time, demand for design skills also explodes, leading to easier access to bite-sized chunks of design expertise.

### Trend Longevity Rating:
*The need for design expertise continues to grow, and this trend is still an important one for any type of organization. In addition, design thinking has exploded as a category of learning and insights. The only nuance here is that the "on-demand" need for design services that this trend predicted has not taken off in the same way.*

**SUBSCRIPTION COMMERCE**

**What's the Trend?**
More businesses and retailers use subscriptions to sell recurring services or products to customers instead of focusing on the one-time sale.

**Trend Longevity Rating:**
*More industries and brands turn to the lessons of subscription commerce, but as I wrote about in this latest trend report – the big shift towards a subscription based business model was too reactionary for some businesses that are now backing away from the model to find something that works better for their situation.*

B-

**INSTANT ENTREPRENEURS**

**What's the Trend?**
As the barriers to starting a new business begin to disappear, incentives and tools mean anyone with an idea can launch a startup knowing that the costs and risks of failure are not as high as they once were.

**Trend Longevity Rating:**
*The shift in many industries from full-time employee to entrepreneur continues to take shape as top professionals continue to branch out on their own. In addition, it is a global priority among national governments to make the process of entrepreneurship faster and easier because there is widespread understanding that entrepreneurs drive economies forward.*

A

**COLLABORATIVE ECONOMY**

**What's the Trend?**
New business models and tools allow consumers and brands to tap the power of sharing and collaborative consumption to find new ways to buy, sell and consume products and services.

**Trend Longevity Rating:**
*While growing last year, the shared or collaborative economy has become one of the more obvious trends anyone could point to today, a symbol of its continued rapid acceleration. While it may be "obvious" now, the impact of it and just how much attention brands are paying to the space justifies its continued ranking among the top trends for its longevity over the years.*

A

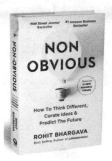

## The 2015 Non-Obvious Trend Report Overview

**Original Publication Date:** *March 1, 2015*
**Original Format:** *Hardcover + eBook*
**Full Book:** *www.nonobviousbook.com/2015*

### THE BACKSTORY

After four years of growing an audience while also solely publishing the Trend Report in digital format, in 2015 I decided to expand. I spent most of the previous year writing about my technique for how I had learned to curate ideas and name trends. I created a "formula" for how anyone could learn to do the same thing, and I published a brand new list of 15 trends as usual. The result was Non-Obvious released as a full length hardcover book for the first time.

The book hit #1 in the entire business category on Amazon and made it up to #27 in ALL Kindle books within 48 hours. The popularity of the book drove it to make the Wall Street Journal Best Seller list the week it launched, but it also introduced the idea of trend curation to a much wider audience. Over the course of the next year, the book was contracted for six translated editions and my speaking and workshops continued – with more global invitations.

### RETROSPECTIVE: HOW ACCURATE WAS THIS REPORT?

The trends that year spotlighted culture in a way that many people started talking about – from *Everyday Stardom* describing how consumer expectation was rising to *Selfie Confidence* describing the role social media plays in building self-esteem. Other trends included *Small Data* – which offered a counter idea to the growing discussions of "big data" and media trends such as *Experimedia* or *Glanceable Content* to describe our shifting attention spans.

# 2015 NON-OBVIOUS TRENDS OVERVIEW – SUMMARY

## WHAT IS A TREND?
*A trend is a unique curated observation about the accelerating present*

### CULTURE & CONSUMER BEHAVIOR - Trends in how we see ourselves and patterns in popular culture

**Everyday Stardom**

**Selfie Confidence**

**Mainstream Mindfulness**

### MARKETING & SOCIAL MEDIA - Trends in how brands are trying to influence and engage consumers

**Branded Benevolence**

**Reverse Retail**

**The Reluctant Marketer**

### MEDIA & EDUCATION - Trends in content and information impacting how we learn or are entertained

**Glanceable Content**

**Mood Matching**

**Experimedia**

### TECHNOLOGY & DESIGN - Trends in technology innovation and product design impacting our behavior

**Unperfection**

**Predictive Protection**

**Engineered Addiction**

### ECONOMICS & ENTREPRENEURSHIP - Trends in business models, startups and careers affecting the future of work or money

**Small Data**

**Disruptive Distribution**

**Microconsumption**

**EVERYDAY STARDOM**

### What's the Trend?
The growth of personalization leads more consumers to expect everyday interactions to be transformed into "celebrity experiences" with them as the stars of the show.

### Trend Longevity Rating:
*As the opportunities for companies to use big data to personalize experiences for customers continue to grow, this expectation from consumers to be treated like superstars has only continued to grow and is even more of a necessity for brands today than it was when this trend was first introduced.*

**SELFIE CONFIDENCE**

### What's the Trend?
The growing ability to share a carefully crafted online persona allows more people to use social content such as selfies as a way to build their own self confidence.

### Trend Longevity Rating:
*Selfies are a misunderstood medium. They were when this trend was first written, and perhaps are even more so today ... yet this trend took the optimistic view that those selfies were an important part of how kids build self-esteem today and that remains true two years later, even as self expression has broadened to include more video and broaden beyond just selfies.*

**MAINSTREAM MINDFULNESS**

### What's the Trend?
Meditation, yoga and quiet contemplation become powerful tools for individuals and organizations to improve performance, health and motivation.

### Trend Longevity Rating:
*Not only is this trend back as one of my featured trends in 2017, but it has now come to describe entire industries, new ways of thinking for organizations and a powerful new movement towards improving ourselves at home and at work.*

# 2015 Marketing & Social Media Trends

**BRANDED BENEVOLENCE**

### What's the Trend?

Companies increasingly put purpose at the center of their businesses to show a deeper commitment to doing good that goes beyond just donating money or getting positive PR.

### Trend Longevity Rating:

*Brands continue to focus on purpose and big initiatives to demonstrate a commitment to the environment, social issues, and ethical business practices. Research continually shows that these commitments matter to customers, employees and even investors – companies will continue to focus on this.*

**REVERSE RETAIL**

### What's the Trend?

Brands increasingly invest in high-touch in-store experiences as a way to build brand affinity and educate customers, while seamlessly integrating with their online channels to complete actual purchases and fulfill orders.

### Trend Longevity Rating:

*The original inspiration for this trend was the rapid growth of "showcase stores" that were being used by brands to offer experiences to consumers with all of the sales made and fulfilled online. Over the years since this trend was first introduced, Louis Vuitton has launched a concept store, Amazon launched a retail bookstore, and there have been plenty of others. The one shift has been that more of these are blending the experiential side with actually selling products like a traditional retail store would.*

**THE RELUCTANT MARKETER**

### What's the Trend?

As marketing shifts away from pure promotion, leaders and organizations abandon traditional silos, embrace content marketing and invest in the customer experience.

### Trend Longevity Rating:

*As content marketing became a greater part of the marketing mix, there were many people running away from describing what they did as "marketing" anymore. This reluctance has equalized somewhat, but the shift behind it away from promotional marketing and toward being useful, providing ultility and answering questions continues to grow.*

**GLANCEABLE CONTENT**

### What's the Trend?
Our shrinking attention spans and the explosion of all forms of content online lead creators to optimize content for rapid consumption at a glance.

### Trend Longevity Rating:
*As much as I would love to say this trend disappeared as people started engaging with content longer (see 2017's Deep Diving trend), this behavior remains true and much of daily or hourly content does need to be glanceable still in order to receive any sort of attention.*

A

---

**MOOD MATCHING**

### What's the Trend?
As tracking technology becomes more sophisticated, media, advertising and immersive experiences like gaming and learning are increasingly tailored to match consumer moods.

### Trend Longevity Rating:
*Automated sentiment filters and new technologies like eye tracking and vocal analysis are letting consumers have even bigger expectations about how technology will cater to them. That said, this trend always described something that was only really relevant in some situations and therefore not as broad or wide-ranging as many of the other trends.*

B

---

**EXPERIMEDIA**

### What's the Trend?
Content creators use social experiments and real life interactions to study human behavior in unique new ways to ultimately build more realistic and entertaining narratives.

### Trend Longevity Rating:
*For a time it seemed that media featuring social experiments was a hot new practice likely to continue for a long time. Over the past few years, though, this trend has slowed down significantly and even though there are still some examples of this happening, it is not at the volumes it once was.*

B

# 2015 Technology & Design Trends

**UNPERFECTION**

### What's the Trend?

As people seek out more personal and human experiences, brands and creators intentionally focus on using personality, quirkiness and intentional imperfections to be more human and desirable.

### Trend Longevity Rating:

*One of my favorite trends for what it described when it was first curated, this trend was partially brought back in this year's trend report along with Lovable Imperfection from 2014. The idea that brands and leaders are showing vulnerability and building trust through their willingness to share flaws is an idea that continues to have resonance.*

- - - - - - - - - - - - - - - - - - - - - - - - - - - - - - - - - - - - - - - - - - -

**PREDICTIVE PROTECTION**

### What's the Trend?

A growing concern for privacy coupled with elevated expectations technology's role in our lives leads to more intuitive products, services and features to help us live better, safer, and more efficient lives.

### Trend Longevity Rating:

*The need for the type of proactive protection that this trend continues to grow each day, and you can see this trend's influence in later predictions from this year's report in particular – such as Robot Renaissance and Self Aware Data. Both trends build upon this one in a way that makes the influence of Predictive Protection as a trend idea continually valuable.*

- - - - - - - - - - - - - - - - - - - - - - - - - - - - - - - - - - - - - - - - - - -

**ENGINEERED ADDICTION**

### What's the Trend?

Greater understanding of the behavioral science behind habit formation leads to more designers and engineers intentionally creating addictive experiences that capture consumers' time, money and loyalty.

### Trend Longevity Rating:

*If you consider the growth of everything from packaged foods to fantasy sports, this trend is still central to how new experiences are conceived and the way that experiences can now be engineered to be irresistible whether they are good for us or not.*

**SMALL DATA**

### What's the Trend?

As consumers increasingly collect their own data from online activities brand-owned big data becomes less valuable than small data.

### Trend Longevity Rating:

*Since the publication of this trend, a best-selling book from Martin Lindstrom of the same title and growing sophistication of technology to personalize experiences has led this trend to be even more relevant today than when it was first curated – so much so that it was one that I narrowly decided against bringing back as part of the 2017 report.*

**DISRUPTIVE DISTRIBUTION**

### What's the Trend?

Creators and makers use new models for distribution to disrupt the usual channels, cut out middlemen, and build more direct connections with fans and buyers.

### Trend Longevity Rating:

*With the news that Amazon may be considering starting a delivery service of its own, Uber is delivering food and the dramatic rise in products being delivered directly without the traditional middleman (such as mattresses), this trend has exploded in recent years and is likely to impact even more industries across 2017.*

**MICROCONSUMPTION**

### What's the Trend?

As new payment models, products and experiences become available in bite-sized portions, multiple industries will experiment with new micro-sized forms of pricing and payments.

### Trend Longevity Rating:

*While there is nothing in this trend that is inherently incorrect or unlikely to continue, it just doesn't have the same type of acceleration behind it as many of the other top rated trends and for that reason I have to rate it lower than the others from this year's report.*

# The 2016 Non-Obvious Trend Report Overview

**Original Publication Date:** *January 25, 2016*
**Original Format:** *Hardcover + eBook*
**Full Book:** *www.nonobviousbook.com/2016*

## THE BACKSTORY

Given the success of the first year that Non-Obvious was available in print (in 2015), this sixth edition of the report had high expectations. For this edition, I decided to publish the book in softcover to make it easier to read (and available at a lower price). Looking backward over the previous trend predictions each year, I also realized that many past predictions still had a lot of relevance for business.

In response, this was the first year I decided to publish ten NEW trends and include five PAST trends in the report (one per category). The past trends would include all new examples as well as my thoughts on what had changed about that trend since it was originally curated and why it deserved to be brought back. The other thing this report featured was an in-depth analysis of the previous year's trends (2015) and how they had evolved over the past year.

## RETROSPECTIVE: HOW ACCURATE WAS THIS REPORT?

Looking back at the previous year is the shortest time frame of all the past trend reports, and so the vast majority of trends are still immediately applicable, current and mostly receive the highest possible rating.

# 2016 NON-OBVIOUS TRENDS OVERVIEW – SUMMARY

## WHAT IS A TREND?
*A trend is a unique curated observation about the accelerating present*

**CULTURE & CONSUMER BEHAVIOR** - Trends in how we see ourselves and patterns in popular culture

**E-mpulse Buying**

**Strategic Downgrading**

**Optimistic Aging**
(Originally Curated 2013)

**MARKETING & SOCIAL MEDIA** - Trends in how brands are trying to influence and engage consumers

**B2Beyond**

**Personality Mapping**

**Branded Utility**
(Originally Curated 2014)

**MEDIA & EDUCATION** - Trends in content and information impacting how we learn or are entertained

**Mainstream Multiculturalism**

**Earned Consumption**

**Anti-Stereotyping**
(Originally Curated 2014)

**TECHNOLOGY & DESIGN** - Trends in technology innovation and product design impacting our behavior

**Virtual Empathy**

**Data Overflow**

**Heroic Design**
(Originally Curated 2013)

**ECONOMICS & ENTREPRENEURSHIP** - Trends in business models, startups and careers affecting the future of work or money

**Insourced Incubation**

**Automated Adulthood**

**Obsessive Productivity**
(Originally Curated 2014)

**E-MPULSE BUYING**

### What's the Trend?

Despite fears that the e-commerce might kill impulse buying, the growing integration of mobile devices into the shopping experience is opening new possibilities for real time marketing to entice consumers to make split second emotional buying decisions once again.

### Trend Longevity Rating:

*Over the past year ecommerce retailers have gotten even more adept at encouraging impulse purchases through their interfaces, and one button ordering is growing in availability. Throughout this year, it is likely more and more retailers will continually add more features designed to encourage impulse buying.*

**STRATEGIC DOWNGRADING**

### What's the Trend?

As more products become Internet-enabled and digitally remastered, consumers start selectively rejecting these supposedly improved products and services – opting to strategically downgrade to simpler, cheaper and sometimes more functional versions instead.

### Trend Longevity Rating:

*A sense of nostalgia remains a high influencing factor for this trend as "retro"products continue to be launched successfully. As newer versions of products and services continue to feel overcomplicated, people will continue to "hack" their own ways to strategically downgrade when it suits their own purposes.*

**OPTIMISTIC AGING**

(Originally Curated 2013)

### What's the Trend?

After years of being sold anti-aging solutions – a generation of newly aging adults are embracing the upside of getting older and finding cause for optimism in the growing opportunities, financial freedom, respect and time that their "third lifetime" can offer.

### Trend Longevity Rating:

*The sense of optimism about what will be achievable in life has remained for the older population but over the past year it was tempered by increasing fears about the macro future of things like the environment, politics, the economy and security. These big issues are casting a distant but significant cloud over the optimism that older people otherwise feel.*

# 2016 Marketing & Social Media Trends

### B2BEYOND MARKETING

**What's the Trend?**
Brands used to promoting their products or services to other businesses embrace their humanity, take inspiration from other sectors and think more broadly about effectively marketing to decision makers as people first, and buyers second.

**Trend Longevity Rating:**
*The steady shift in B2B marketing best practices is continuing to take shape thanks to a small number of highly influential advertisers. As more brands look to the examples of GE, Intel and IBM – they are increasingly inspired to create more marketing that is simultaneously more fun, broad, relevant and strategic.*

### PERSONALITY MAPPING

**What's the Trend?**
As behavioral measurement tools build a detailed map of our personalities, multiple industries will be able to use this information to bring likeminded people together and provide more transformative learning and bonding experiences.

**Trend Longevity Rating:**
*There is no doubt that organizations are getting much better at using the data that they have to better understand consumer personalities and cater to those. As this data translates into things like customer journey maps and personas, the trend of matching communications to consumer personality will continue.*

### BRANDED UTILITY

**What's the Trend?**
Brands begin to focus on a combination of content marketing and a greater integration between marketing and operations to provide value through usefulness in customer's lives.

**Trend Longevity Rating:**
*As content marketing explodes, this trend is undeniably going along with it. The idea that brands can and should provide more utility for their potential customers is leading brands to invest in creating quality content, shifting marketing spending and creating a revolution within marketing that shows no signs of slowing down.*

**MAINSTREAM MULTICULTURALISM**

**What's the Trend?**
After years of being ignored, niche demographics, multicultural citizens and their cultures find new widespread acceptance through a growing integration of diverse ideas and people in entertainment, products and politics.

**Trend Longevity Rating:**
*Even as xenophobic political sentiment lingers in many places around the world, the generational shift towards acceptance and embrace of multiple cultures is allowing this trend to have a continued impact in the business, art, media and culture of today.*

. . . . . . . . . . . . . . . . . . . . . . . . . . . . . . . . . . . . . . . . . . . . . . . . . . . . . . . . . . . . .

**EARNED CONSUMPTION**

**What's the Trend?**
The desire for authentic experiences leads to a willingness from consumers to earn their right to consume, offering businesses a chance to build more loyalty and engagement by letting consumers "pay" for products or services with more than just money..

**Trend Longevity Rating:**
*There are still many situations where consumers want to earn their chance to be a customer and feel the pride in achieving their place - yet a growing skepticism of experiences and products means that anyone selling anything has to work harder to meet the bar of whether they are even worth the time before a consumer will engage. This trend still has impact, but only selectively.*

. . . . . . . . . . . . . . . . . . . . . . . . . . . . . . . . . . . . . . . . . . . . . . . . . . . . . . . . . . . . .

**ANTI-STEREOTYPING**
(Originally Curated 2014)

**What's the Trend?**
A fundamental change takes place across media and culture, where traditional gender roles are being reversed, assumptions about alternative lifestyles are challenged, and perceptions of what makes someone belong to a particular gender, ethnicity, or category are being upended.

**Trend Longevity Rating:**
*The number of people who now define themselves with something other than the traditional descriptors of male or female is growing every day. As a result, this trend has become even more critical as a way to understand and react to the sentiment by avoiding any accidental stereotyping in communications or recruiting new talent.*

# 2016 Technology & Design Trends

**VIRTUAL
EMPATHY**

**What's the Trend?**
An improved quality and lower costs for virtual reality allows creators to tell more immersive stories and let people see the world from another point of view – growing their empathy in the process.

**Trend Longevity Rating:**
*If there was a higher grade than A to give, this trend would most likely earn it. Over the coming year, the examples of how virtual reality will be used to engage, improve and quantify human empathy will probably become too numerous to count. If virtual reality is truly an empathy machine, 2017 will be the year this machine moves our entire culture forward.*

**DATA
OVERFLOW**

**What's the Trend?**
The combination of growing personal and corporate owned data mixed with open data creates a new challenge for companies to go beyond algorithms for data management and rely on better artificial intelligence, smarter curation, and more startup investment.

**Trend Longevity Rating:**
*Data continues to "overflow" and create problems of measurement and analysis, but as the latest 2017 data trend (Self-Aware Data) shows, the overflow is no longer the same challenge it once was because of greater automation of data and the ability to act in real time based on this automation.*

**HEROIC DESIGN**
(Originally Curated 2013)

**What's the Trend?**
Design takes a leading role in the introduction of new products, ideas, and inspiration to change the world in nuanced, audacious, irreverent, and sometimes unexpectedly heroic ways.

**Trend Longevity Rating:**
*The continued presence of design competitions to celebrate new solutions for global problems and a suite of tools to help anyone bring more design thinking to their own jobs means that this trend of putting design on a pedestal and asking it (and designers) to create "heroic" solutions will continue.*

**INSOURCED
INCUBATION**

**What's the Trend?**
Companies desperate to bring more innovation into their enterprise turn to a new model of intrapreneurship modeled after the best business incubators—bringing innovators in house, providing support and resources, and starting innovation labs.

**Trend Longevity Rating:**
*The slate of Innovation Labs and new efforts chronicled as part of the writeup for this trend are now starting to produce early results. These early successes will legitimize the idea of this trend and cause more investment and attention from organizations into creating their own programs in this space.*

**AUTOMATED
ADULTHOOD**

**What's the Trend?**
As more people go through a prolonged period of emerging adulthood, a growing range of technology and services help to automate all aspects of their journey to adulthood.

**Trend Longevity Rating:**
*If there was any doubt that this trend was describing something significant, just look at the advent of new tracking products to measure everything about life, co-living arrangements and other facilities that ensure people have partners to help carry the emotionally and physically into adulthood.*

**OBSESSIVE
PRODUCTIVITY**
(Originally Curated 2014)

**What's the Trend?**
Thanks to our reduced attention spans and "always-on technology", a built-in necessity to be productive in every moment is rapidly evolving into an obsession that underpins every brand interaction or other experience they have.

**Trend Longevity Rating:**
*To say that technology has made us all hyper aware of those moments when our time is valued or wasted would be even more of an understatement than when this trend was originally written 3 years ago. Productivity is still an obsession – and looks to stay that way.*

# AFTERWORD

Apparently, the world will end on March 16, 2880.

While putting the final touches on this book, I came across a news article about a team of scientists who discovered a 0.3% chance the world will end on that day due to a cosmic collision course between the Earth and a celestial body known only as Asteroid 1950 DA.

The story immediately struck me as the perfect metaphor for the types of predictions we commonly encounter … overblown proclamations with dire consequences and relatively little certainty.

One of my aims throughout this book was to challenge the lazy or obvious trend predictions that are published each year. They are sadly similar to this exaggerated astronomical example in terms of the lack of value they offer us in the present.

**A real trend is a unique curated observation of the accelerating present.**

So this book very specifically doesn't offer geopolitical arguments for why Denmark is going to become the world's next superpower by 2050 thanks to wind energy production, or optimistic technology predictions about how self-driving cars will enable virtual-reality tourism during daily commutes.

I know those kinds of predictions are sexy, and some might even come true thanks to pure chance. Unfortunately, they also include a lot of uncertainty. Getting better at observing reality means preparing for the future should involve far less guesswork.

Curating trends is certainly about seeing the things other don't. Yet it is also more broadly about a mindset that encourages you to be curious and thoughtful. It is about techniques that help you move from trying to be a speed reader to being a speed understander, as Isaac Asimov would say.

I believe the future belongs to those who can learn to use their powers of observation to see the connections between industries, ideas and behaviors and curate them into a deeper understanding of the world around us.

I'm not saying that type of thinking can save us from the asteroid 867 years from now – but it can definitely change the way we approach our lives and our businesses in *the present*.

Preparing for the future starts with understanding today, as it always has.

# ACKNOWLEDGEMENTS

The concept for the book has been many years in the making – and now that it is officially an annual series with a new update every year, the first group of people I need to thank are the many people who have read an earlier edition of this book or one of my Non-Obvious Trend Reports and decided to get in touch and interact with me directly.

As much as anyone, this book is for them – and if you happen to be among that group, I want to thank you first.

Aside from this broad group, there are also some individuals who helped with various stages of getting this book (and previous editions) ready for publication and deserve my specific thanks:

First of all, to Paresh for jumping into the process of trend curation, working on the ideas for this year, becoming a true partner and just being a force for good. You are the original Lifter.

To Matthew for being a sounding board on the editorial process and jumping in to provide assistance when needed on updates and ever increasing list of previous trends.

To Frank, Anton, and Jessica for all your design smarts and making the visual design of the book as beautiful as it is, and to the entire design team at Faceout for the original inspiration and setting the tone for the series back in the beginning.

To Marleen and her international team for helping to bring the ideas in Non-Obvious to so many diverse audiences around the world in their own language.

To Marnie for all your work keeping this, and so many other, Ideapress projects on track.

To Rich for being a great partner, always working under a crazy timeline and still getting things done like a pro.

To my wife Chhavi, who continually manages to deal with a shifting annual writing process that requires me to disappear to finish off chapters and "visualize" ideas by spreading my notes across entire rooms of the house. You are the first person to tell me when it's good and the first to tell me when it isn't. I love that.

And finally, to my boys Rohan and Jaiden for remaining curious enough about the world to continually inspire me to observe more, judge less and always listen with both ears.

From time to time, we all need a reminder like that.

# RESEARCH:
## Notes, References, & Credits

—

The preparation of this book and Trend Report involves consulting hundreds of publications, interviewing dozens of experts and reviewing more than 50 books each year.

The first year I published Non-Obvious in print format – I decided to include every reference used in the researching of this book in a chapter by chapter list. The vast majority of the research contained referral links, but it added an unnecessary 20 pages of extra bulk to the book which most readers didn't use.

Instead of that, this issue of Non-Obvious will follow the process from last year and include all the references online in a downloadable PDF with active links which you can access from the URL below:

**WWW.NONOBVIOUSBOOK.COM/RESOURCES**

# INDEX

video, 104
Blue Apron, 95
Blue Frog Robotics, 154
Blue Man Group, 181
Bluetooth Low Energy (BLE), 139
Blume, Judy, 135
Body language, interpreting, 26
Body Shop, 170
Boeing, 150, 151
Bohr, Neils, 209
Bollick, Kate, 70, 71
Bolthouse Farms, 198
Bonding, seeking out mindful moments for, 192
Bookstores, Argentinan love for, 134–135
Bosch, 161
Bounty, 96
Boys, comparison of playing by, with girls, 180–181
Brainful media, consuming, 22
Brainless media, 22
Brain Pickings (Popova), 30
Branded benevolence, 240, 242
Branded inspiration, 224, 226
Branded utility, 232, 234, 248, 250
Brands
history of, 118–120
switching between, 93
Brand Storytelling Trend Workshop, 202–203
Branson, Richard, 27, 81, 176
"Breaking Bad," 111
Breazeal, Cynthia, 152
Brexit vote, 177
Brinker, Hans, Budget Hotel, 112–113
Brockman, John, 23
Buffett, Warren, 80, 179, 186
Burt's Bees, 170
Business Strategy Trend Workshop, 203

C
Café effect, 86
Caiozzo, Paul, 75
Carell, Steve, 131
Carter, Tom, 145
Case, Jean, 172
Case Foundation, 172
Casper mattress, 187
Cat & Jack, 180
Cats, 181
Caudalie, 170
Certain future, short-term, ii
Certainty, dangers of false, 60

Chan, Jackie, 112
Charles Schwab, 159
ChatBots, 154–155
Cherokee (brand), 180
Chicago Toy and Game Fair tradeshow, 136
Children, explaining the world to, 25
Cincinnati, as Industry 4.0 Demonstration City, 162
Circle, 89
Circo (brand), 180
Cisco Systems, 81
The Click Moment (Johansson), 198–199
Coca-Cola, 27, 51, 80, 104, 119, 198
Cohen, Boyd, 144
Collaborative economy, 232, 237
Collectivist cultures, 76
Colloquy, 93
Columbus, Christopher, 22
Company Culture Trend Workshop, 203
Complications, curated, 23–24
Concept homes, 168
Concepts
seeking, 43
summarizing, 43
Content marketing, 219
The Cool Hunter, 207
Cool Hunting, 206–207
Copeland, Misty, 69
Cornell, Brian, 180
Corporate wellness, 188–189
Correa, Sergio Juárez, 125
Cosmetics, brands in, 170–171
Cosmetics app, 171
Costolo, Dick, 81
Courvoisier, 119
Covert, Abby, 28
Cranley, John, 162
Creativity, lack of, 14
Crispin Porter + Bogusky (CP + B), 198
Crowdfunding, 152
Culture and Consumer Behavior Trends
Desperate Detox, 65, 85–91
Fierce Femininity, 65, 67–74
Side Quirks, 65, 75–83
Culture books, creating, 137
Curation
defined, 7
goal of, 19
non-obvious trends, 56–59
rise of, 19–20
Curationism (Balzer), 19–20
Curations

# ABOUT THE AUTHOR

Rohit Bhargava is a trend curator, marketing expert, storyteller and the Wall Street Journal best-selling author of five books on topics as wide ranging as the future of business and why leaders never eat cauliflower. Rohit is the founder of the Influential Marketing Group (IMG) and The Non-Obvious Company, teaches marketing and pitching at Georgetown University and has been invited to speak in 32 countries around the world. Prior to becoming an entrepreneur and going independent, Rohit spent 15 years leading brand strategy at two of the largest marketing agencies in the world (Ogilvy and Leo Burnett), advising some of the largest brands in the world. He lives in the Washington DC area with his wife and two boys.

# ALSO BY THE AUTHOR

 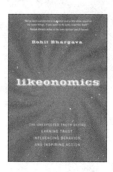 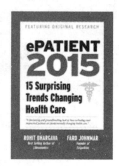